"NEVER GIVE IN, NEVER GIVE UP"

A MEMOIR OF HOPE

by

EUGENE F. ELANDER

ISBN: 9781988557328

Published Year: 2023
Published Location: Published in the United States of America
Published by: Three Ravens Media

*FLAG DAY THOUGHTS ON BECOMING AN
AMERICAN SWEDE – June 6, 2022:*

"Du Gamla, Du Fria" – You Old Land, and Free:
That anthem has come to mean so much to me!
First, as visitor, then as resident, for many a year –
With Birgit's great family, good friends, and much cheer –
And now, ultimate honor has been granted to me:
Thanks to my new nation: an American Swede I can be!

**This memoir is dedicated to my beloved Birgit –
and to her son Thomas, whom I have now joined
by also becoming an American Swede.**

*Eugene F. Elander, Visby, Gotland,
Sweden, Summer 2022*

*About the Title: Upon reaching the half-century mark at the age
of fifty, now thirty-five years ago, the author decided it was time
to adopt a motto guiding the remainder of his life.*

NEVER GIVE IN,
NEVER GIVE UP
is that motto & theme.

In loving memory of
my Polish cousin, Sorella Goldsobel

Birth: 13 Nov 1934 (per Ancestry.com)
Warsaw, Mazowieckie, Poland
Death: Sep 1942 (aged 7)
Warsaw, Mazowieckie, Poland
Burial: Treblinka Holocaust Memorial,
Powiat ostrowski, Mazowieckie, Poland
ID 127888697 ·

Sorella was the daughter of Basia and Leon Goldsobel. Before WWII began thousands of Jews lived in Poland; most lived in Warsaw. The Nazis invaded Poland in 1939. The Jews were forced to wear the yellow star. In Oct. 1940 Sorella, and her mother and older sister were forced to leave their homes and live in a run-down area in the city. In Nov. 1940, like most Jews, they were forced to be sealed in the ghetto and forbidden to leave. Conditions were crowded and unsanitary, and caused starvation. In September 1942, Sorella and her family were caught in a Nazi raid in the ghetto. They were sent to freight trucks in the Warsaw ghetto. Upon arrival they were selected for extermination. Sorella was sent to the gas chambers. She was only seven years old when her life was ended. RIP, Sorella Goldsobel. NEVER AGAIN!

*　　　*　　　*

The Romanov Connection to the Goldsobel Family, and through them, to author Eugene F. Elander

I am named after my great-grand-uncle Dr. Ullich Goldsobel of Warsaw, Poland, who served as a physician to the last Romanov Czar of All the Russias, Czar Nicholas II, later executed with his entire family by the Bolsheviks in 1918 in the basement of their Summer Palace at Yekaterinburg. According to my family history, in the early 1900s Ullich had a brief affair with Czarina Alexandra, while Czar Nicholas II was hunting, before returnimg to Warsaw with a secret son who had resulted from the union. That child was raised as a Goldsobel, and would have become my own grand-uncle, perhaps making me one of the last living Romanovs. The details may be myth or family history.

"NEVER GIVE IN, NEVER GIVE UP":
A MEMOIR OF HOPE

FOREWORD

Every life has many defining moments. Some are personal – finding a soul mate, the birth of a child, the loss of parents. Some are national – the ending of World War II and later conflicts, the Kennedy and King assassinations, the first moon landing. And some are societal – far too many prime defining moments of this brave new Millennium have resulted from acts of terrorism, new diseases, and now an invasion. This 21st Century has had a rough start.

What such defining moments have in common is that they represent **change.** Unfortunately, as we well know, not all changes are for the better. Nor are needed changes easy to achieve. This book focuses on a host of changes: personal, national, and societal – including changes which have occurred in the recent past, and those which are vitally needed for the immediate future.

Although significantly autobiographical (with some names changed, to protect the innocent – or the guilty, in a few cases), our focus goes beyond the personal level. The descriptions of events, agencies, and individuals are factual. The nuclear submarine incident occurred; only some names have been changed. Of greatest importance, the Centurion and SCOPE Programs are real, valid, and timely. Those programs, detailed in the Appendices to this book, along with several other counter-terrorism and hazard mitigation recommendations which emerge from this book, are vitally needed to help ensure our society's safety and security. And they are needed **at once.** We must learn fully the lessons of the 20th Century, and now of Ukraine: *Security, like liberty, requires both eternal vigilance & effective action.*

The ancient Romans asked the question: *Who will watch the watchers?*

In our own age, we must ask a further question: *Who will turn the tides?* Each of us can play a role in answering both of these questions. The manner in which we answer them, the forms of our responses – the challenges of maintaining our basic humanity in the face of grave inhumanity – all will determine the quality of our lives, and the fate of future generations as well. **This book is dedicated to believing in a future which we can reach, and to reaching a future in which we can believe. Indeed, we must never give in and never give up!** *Meanwhile, we must maintain faith and hope!*

Eugene F. Elander, Summer 2022, Visby, Gotland, Sweden & SoCal, USA

CHAPTER ONE

◆

BEGINNINGS

I must confess to being an unlikely recruit into the world of intelligence work and counter-terrorism. Of course, perhaps the best recruits are the unlikely ones. What makes my case unusual, though, is that my recruiter was Israeli spymaster Isser Harel himself – the man who captured the notorious Nazi Adolph Eichmann, author of Hitler's "Final Solution" which murdered six million of my people. Perhaps even more unusual are the concrete plans and programs which I developed to prevent and reduce terrorism, particularly terrorist incidents directed against the United States – and how very hard it has been to get those plans and programs considered, let alone implemented in the USA.

Although I am a native New Yorker, from Jamaica, Queens, to be precise, my family had moved to Dayton, Ohio, when my father was promoted to sales manager of his firm, United Aircraft Products, which was based in Dayton. We had moved to what was then South Dayton, later renamed Kettering in honor of early automotive pioneer Charles Kettering, whose best-known accomplishment was the invention of the self-starter. My last two years of high school were completed at Fairmont High School there, where I also joined an explorer scout troop and began to enjoy hiking, camping, and even cliff and mountain climbing, ultimately via trips across North America to the Canadian Rockies.

Of course, these pleasurable high school and extracurricular activities had to end with graduation. That fall, I headed East to Boston with my friend Karl; we were the two Fairmont graduates admitted to the Massachusetts Institute of Technology in Cambridge that year. Karl and I drove to MIT in his aunt's old Hudson, which had such a profound tendency to overheat that our speed was limited not by posted speed limits, but rather by the car's temperature gauge.

After two years at MIT, though, I found I was not well suited to engineering. I was learning more and more about less and less, and eventually would know a great deal about nothing, as I thought of it. MIT's required military training did not encourage me to stay, either, as I found I detested the regimentation and control exercised by the ROTC over us cadets. Like many other Techies, I had trouble taking the ROTC seriously, and we often found ways of undercutting that military program. For example, on Parade Day, when we were all supposed to strut our stuff under review by military officials, a group of us arranged for Strauss waltzes to be played over every "hi fi" system in the dormitory adjacent to the parade ground, drowning out all the military commands.

Then, there was the "loyalty oath" which all student cadets had to sign under penalty of expulsion from MIT for refusing to do so. My first act of rebellion was to question the wording of that loyalty oath, demanding that I have the opportunity to study it at length. I took a copy with me, and then conveniently forgot to ever sign it.

Like many other young people in that era, I had been convinced by my high school guidance counselor that it was my patriotic duty to become an engineer, so that we could beat the Soviets in the "space race" to the moon and perhaps beyond. Upon deciding that the Soviets would just have to be defeated without me, I left MIT and enrolled at Bowling Green State University as a business major. This allowed me to live at home on most weekends, socialize with my friends who were still in the area, and take many courses which were really of interest. What BGSU did not do, however, was to qualify me for any interesting job or career.

While I had worked summers at my father's aircraft company in Dayton, the ROTC experience convinced me that I did not want to become part o f the "military-industrial complex." That phrase had been coined by President Dwight Eisenhower, in a perhaps surprising but prophetic warning he issued to the nation – a warning to be wary of the growing power of the mega-corporations. Thus, upon my graduation from BGSU with honors, and with the encouragement of faculty there, I decided upon further study. The University of Pennsylvania accepted me as a graduate student in economics, and even offered me a teaching assistant post at its Wharton School. For the next four years, I studied in Philadelphia, with no time for much else. Graduate school was quite demanding, as we had the best and brightest economics students from all over the world, and there was intense competition. I loved my time at Penn, and teaching at Wharton.

In my last year of graduate school, my father died quite suddenly of a heart attack. He had never previously been ill – but, feeling "under the weather," he went into the hospital for a checkup. While there, a blood clot lodged in a heart artery and killed him. Late at night, our family lawyer called to tell me of the tragedy, and I rushed home to be with my mother in Dayton, and then to attend his funeral in New York. Up until that time, I had believed that my parents were invulnerable; after dad's premature demise, I became both more pessimistic and more realistic at the same time. I had learned that life could be fleeting and could end suddenly – therefore, one had to make the most of each moment.

After returning to Penn to complete my final year of graduate school, as my father would have wished me to do, I moved back to Dayton to help my mother, particularly as I was an only child and she did not drive. I began to teach at Miami University of Ohio, which opened a new campus the following year right in Dayton, later named Wright State University. The fledgling school had been named after Dayton's aviation pioneers, the Wright Brothers, who mostly had built bicycles there. Wilbur and Orville Wright had to go to Kitty Hawk, North Carolina, to fly the world's first real airplane, partly because in Dayton they were seen as lunatics for believing they could build a "flying machine."

After a few years at this new campus, I was lured to nearby Antioch College by the school's offer of a tenure-track assistant professorship.

The lively social life Antioch offered was also attractive, in that "hippie" era of long hair and free love. I had been appointed Assistant Professor of Administration, as the word Business would not have been popular preceding the word Administration at Antioch, which was quite a radical institution.

It was while teaching at Antioch that I first encountered the world of intelligence agencies. My department chair and I did not get along well, and it became clear that for me there would be no tenure at the end of my track. I had discovered that Antioch was far more permissive towards its students than towards its faculty. So it was time to find a new position, perhaps even outside of teaching, as I felt ready to spread my wings. Then, I happened to see a blind ad in a professional journal looking for writers of tracts and articles on economics.

Having just purchased one of the first new Mustang convertibles, I drove up to Ann Arbor, Michigan, home of the University of Michigan, for an interview. I had assumed that the vague want-ad to which I had responded was probably posted by some institute affiliated with that University. However, when I got to the street address given in the interview invitation letter I had received after applying, I found only a small dry-cleaning establishment. Entering this shop, I asked for the person who was to interview me, and without further ado the proprietor took me through a curtain in the rear of the shop, then knocked three times on a heavy door which was opened by a young man with close-cropped hair, a style which was unusual then. The proprietor returned to his duties, the door closed, and the interviewer and I were alone.

CHAPTER TWO

◆

INTERVIEW

I gave my name to the man in the back room, who replied saying "call me Ken", no last name given, and the first name spoken in such a way that I was not sure if it was his real name. Ken invited me to sit down on a hard chair while he went behind a cluttered desk and asked me about myself.

Since my department chair at Antioch was unlikely to provide a good letter of reference, I had already decided that my best bet was to level with the interviewer. Upon stating that I was ready to do something other than teach, Ken said that this was one reason I had been chosen to be interviewed; the other reason involved some writing samples on economic themes which I had submitted with my resume.

Ken then asked how I would feel about writing articles and even books on the capitalist system and the market economy, suitable for translation into several unspecified languages. At that point, it dawned upon me that one of those languages was likely to be Russian, which I asked about pointedly. Ken confirmed that, indeed, my work would be translated into Russian and other Eastern European languages, and that it would have to be slanted to glorify the virtues of capitalism and why it was far better than communism. My potential employer would provide the topics and themes for my writing. Since my minor in graduate school had been comparative economic systems, I began to see more clearly why I was being considered for such a job. But there were some conditions, which Ken then explained to me.

My writing would be anonymous, no name would appear on any work I produced. Some shorter pieces might be read over Radio Free Europe, and it was possible that I would become a "ghost writer" for some American diplomat or other public official. If my work was effective in the fight against Communism, I could expect a long and fruitful career with the unnamed agency represented by Ken (by then, I believed it was the CIA). I might even be promoted to "field work" according to Ken; when I asked the nature of such field work, Ken smiled and said, "All in good time."

But I found that I was not having such a "good time" regarding the interview; the work opportunity being presented was nothing more nor less than propaganda production, and in my naïve view, such work was improper and deceitful. I recalled the famous adage of George Bernard Shaw, namely that "the difference between capitalism and communism was that in capitalism man exploits man, whereas in communism it's the other way around." There was no way I would ever become a party to such propaganda production; let each system stand or fall on its own merits, but let it be presented fully and fairly. Of course, I could not say anything like that to Ken, so I had to stall for time – and then just get out of there.

I managed to stumble through the rest of the interview, telling Ken I would have to think over the opportunity offered, since it was such a departure from my past work. As I drove the six hours back to Dayton from Ann Arbor, I began to think about why I had had such a strong negative reaction to Ken's proposal. It suddenly came to me that there was more involved than my distaste for propaganda; my father's untimely death had been on my mind, even if perhaps not consciously considered during the interview.

My father had become more and more aggravated by conditions at his executive job in the military aircraft industry; his company was involved with getting contracts out of the Pentagon, often by techniques which amounted to discreet bribery. I knew, for example, that the company frequently showed Pentagon military brass and procurement officers a good time via a hotel suite maintained for that purpose, well stocked with booze, women, and such entertainments as poker games. My father frequently took dignitaries to the Beverly Hills Country Club, an illegal gambling den in Northern Kentucky, just across the Ohio River from Cincinnati. In fact, on occasion I had been invited to go along on these junkets. Once I understood the nature of these arrangements, and that they represented a quid-pro-quo for defense contracts, I had let my father know what I thought of such improprieties. Surprisingly, he told me he did not like them either – but that was how the military aircraft procurement business was done.

While there was thus no way I would even consider joining Ken and his comrades (perhaps a poor choice of term) in their efforts to make the world safer for America, I still had the problem of likely non-reappointment as an assistant professor at Antioch. For a few weeks, I tried to "stroke" my department chair – but it became increasingly clear that I would be given notice of non-renewal at Antioch, either at the end of this present contract year, or perhaps with a terminal one-year contract if the school wanted to be kind. I did not want to accept such kindness; at small colleges, bad news travels fast, and I had no doubt that I would become a pariah before the end of that academic year.

Deciding that it was time to move back East, now that my widowed mother was planning to return to New York, I began a serious job search, deciding that I would not accept any appointment below the rank of associate professor, which would actually be a promotion. But such jobs were not easy to find, especially late in the school year. Still, there were a few openings, and I used an academic placement agency staffed with top "head hunters" to find such an opportunity. After several weeks of searching by the agency, an available business department chairmanship was located at a new college in Mays Landing, Southern New Jersey, serving the Atlantic County-Atlantic City area. The new job location led to a new chapter of my life, with some surprising twists and turns!

CHAPTER THREE

◆

ATLANTIC COUNTY

Bidding a not-so-fond farewell to Antioch and to Ohio, I moved to Brigantine, New Jersey, over the summer, beginning my duties as Business Department Chair at Atlantic College that fall. The college was brand new then, located in the pine barrens about a half hour West of the shore, and I was a member of the "charter faculty" as we were then called. The campus consisted of several low yellow-brick buildings, and some campus roads were not even paved yet. I was assigned the supervision of about a dozen full and part-time business and economics teachers, as well as steering my division through the college's initial accreditation. During that first year, I had time for little more than work.

Having always had the dream of living on a lake or bay, I had found a house on West Shore Drive in Brigantine, a fairly large island just North of Atlantic City, to which Brigantine was connected by a causeway and bridge. The island was relatively under-populated then, with a four-mile-long undeveloped beach at the far end and a lot of open space remaining elsewhere. In the spring, sea turtles would come up to lay their eggs in the abundant sand. Brigantine was then truly lovely, a "jewel on the South Jersey shore." But our new island was a threatened location.

Atlantic City, Brigantine's neighbor, had been "sin city" for many decades, ever since its decline as a summer watering hole for New Yorkers and Philadelphians. In the old days, my parents and I had spent several weeks each summer at Atlantic City's Claridge Hotel, until we moved to

Ohio. Atlantic City's elegant hotels, outstanding shops and restaurants like Captain Starn's, and the annual Miss America pageant had made Atlantic City a vacation treasure. But America was changing, and so was Atlantic City, which was in the process of turning into the vice center of the Northeast. Illegal gambling was available at the Elks Club, drugs and prostitutes were available along the Boardwalk and adjacent Atlantic and Pacific Avenues, and political corruption was commonplace and largely overlooked.

Perhaps none of these undesirable aspects of Atlantic City would have impacted me had I not determined to start a hotel-motel management program through my department at Atlantic College. Having studied the area even before moving there, I had noted a real shortage of solid well-paying jobs with career paths. There seemed to be very significant labor exploitation in South Jersey; and when I raised the need to do something about it with college administrators, I was usually told, "well, that's the way it's always been." However, those same administrators agreed to introduce my proposed program in hotel-motel management as part of our business curriculum. Thus, I hoped to provide students with both job opportunities and a real career path attuned to the needs of this special area.

Naturally, such a community-based program needed to have an advisory committee, and I recruited a number of top executives in the local recreation and entertainment fields to serve on that committee. What I did not realize was that most of my recruits were connected in one way or another with the rackets so popular in Atlantic City. Indeed, some of my "superstars" on the advisory committee turned out to be capos and even higher officials of the Philadelphia organized crime syndicate. These members then recommended others of their ilk to serve on the committee, so that, unknown to me, it soon turned into an arm of the Philadelphia and New York crime syndicates.

Probably, none of those facts would have come to light were it not for the initial overtures aimed at having legalized gambling come to Atlantic City. The gambling interests were then only beginning to make the case for a Las Vegas East, allegedly to save that crumbling city. It would take some years, and a lot of money spread around in the right political and other places, before gambling casinos would be approved for Atlantic City – but the groundwork was already being put in place, and I unknowingly became a major obstacle to that groundwork…

The casino interests had been putting out feelers to Atlantic College for some kind of endorsement of legalized gambling as an economic development project. Besides the general pressure on our President and Deans, I had been approached via the hotel-motel advisory committee, using the pretext of job creation and income enhancement for the entire area. Having been to Las Vegas several times, I found that city to be crime ridden, corrupt, and ruled by the mob. I did not want Atlantic City to turn into another Vegas. Further, my analysis showed that while casino gambling would raise significant revenue for the State of New Jersey, very little of that revenue would end up helping Atlantic City. Rather, funds would be diverted elsewhere, while the poor city would have to absorb the costs of much more police and fire protection, crime prevention, addiction services, and the other inevitable costs of major gambling operations. So, I was strongly opposed to having casino gambling come anywhere near Atlantic County, and I said so.

Meanwhile, I had become a member, and then an officer, of the Brigantine Jaycees. It was always good form for college staff to become involved in their communities – but in addition, the realtor who had sold me my home on the Inland Waterway was a Jaycees' vice president who recruited me for the civic group. We met on a weekly basis at the Brigantine Country Club, and I took on several responsibilities for the Jaycees, such as program chair and fund-raising organizer. Indeed, I was selected by the New Jersey Jaycees as an Outstanding Young Man of America in my second year in Brigantine.

The next fall, I was asked to chair the program for the New Jersey Regional Jaycees annual convention, which brought together all of the clubs in South Jersey, usually at the Atlantic City Convention Center. Putting the conference program together required the selection of outstanding and inspirational speakers, who were supposed to motivate members to new levels of achievement, as well as to doing more for each club. My pick for keynote speaker was a crusading prosecuting attorney who was unalterably opposed to legalized gambling and made a strong case against casinos expanding beyond Las Vegas. Little did I know whose toes I was stepping on, until the Regional Jaycees Board vetoed my choice of speaker as too "controversial". This really meant that the gambling interests who had permeated the Jaycees, as they had done with my advisory committee, would not tolerate any anti-gambling crusaders speaking at the annual convention. While I reluctantly accepted the Board's decision, in my naivete, I did not really understand it.

Nor did I understand then that, by even recommending an anti-gambling keynote speaker, I had indeed sealed my fate in South Jersey; the next day, the dean at Atlantic College called me into his office to tell me that I was not to be reappointed as Business Division chair! I went at once to the college president's office – and he then confirmed the decision, while refusing to give any reason for ending my key role at Atlantic College. Something smelled very bad about the entire situation, particularly as the news leaked out to both faculty and students, along with solid reports that three other named "troublemakers" were getting the boot. The next issue of the student newspaper carried a cartoon showing the faces of all four of us outgoing faculty members, with this caption: MOUNT SHUSHFOUR – and a college-wide assembly convened to protest terminations!

CHAPTER FOUR

◆

NEW DIRECTIONS?

That night, I could not sleep, mostly thinking about my damaged career – first, I had left Antioch College due to mutual unhappiness between me and my department chair; now, I would be leaving Atlantic College for unfair and then-unclear reasons. I did not yet understand that I had broken the unwritten rules in Atlantic County by opposing the power structure, and now I would pay the price and the piper. All of this was a very depressing prospect, but one which led me to seek real alternatives and new directions.

One of the advantages of being a department chair was that I had a reduced teaching load, and had that next day free, as it was a Friday. I usually made no appointments on Fridays so that I could enjoy a three-day weekend and rest up from the hectic week. Now, by seven in the morning, I was on the Garden State Parkway headed North towards New York. The choice of time was not so good, however, as I ran into the morning working traffic into the city. I decided to leave my car at the Newark bus station and take a bus to the Port of New York Authority terminal just below Times Square, so that I could then walk to the Israeli Consulate. I had a plan in mind for a totally new direction in my life.

Arriving in New York shortly before noon, I got off the bus from Newark, avoiding the unpleasant aspects of the terminal (homeless people sleeping in corners, litter, and worse) and emerging into an overcast New York City day. I headed East on 42nd street, long before a later mayor managed to clean up the area, passing a host of sleazy porn theaters and similar attractions. I had lunch at my favorite eating place when I was by myself in the City that Never Sleeps – Tad's Steak House between Broadway and Seventh Avenue, with an excellent sirloin steak, salad, roll and iced tea at a very affordable price. After lunch, I continued to the Israeli consulate at 800 Second Avenue, showing my ID and stating that I wanted to volunteer as an economist for Israel.

I was referred to an Israeli official, after the receptionist greeted me with "Shalom" and said someone would be down to meet me. A few minutes later, a small middle-aged man arrived and escorted me to an office upstairs, stating, "I am here to answer your questions. Then, if you still wish to proceed, you will be instructed as to immigration to Israel. First, though, we need to know why you are considering leaving America."

I replied that I was a great admirer of the fledgling State of Israel, after following the lengthy United Nations debate over the creation of a Jewish homeland. I closed my rather-lengthy commentary with the words of Senator Robert Kennedy, who had been murdered, ironically allegedly for his support for Israel, while running for President, "Some people see things as they are, and ask, Why? I see things as they might be, and ask, Why not?" Yes, I was fully prepared to do what this new nation required, as long as I was not being disloyal to the United States, which did not appear to be the case.

The Israeli official's response, however, surprised me – he smiled while stating that Israel already had all the economists needed, perhaps even too many, and I could not expect to serve in that capacity. Rather, what Israel really needed was more high school teachers in the new "development towns", including English teachers; would I accept such a post, understanding that my first task would be to learn spoken Hebrew fluently?

I was far from prepared to accept Israel's offer to make me a high school teacher, having read about the development towns being in such locations as the Negev Desert, where they were being carved from the wilderness, quite far from Jerusalem or Tel Aviv. I told the Israeli official that I would think about this opportunity, and headed back home.

CHAPTER FIVE

◈

AFTERMATH

Returning to Atlantic County, New Jersey, I quietly began to make plans to leave my post at Atlantic College – vowing that I would not leave quietly. Thus, my primary effort was not the seeking of a new job. Rather, I sought a young, crusading attorney who had vowed to oppose casino gambling for Atlantic City. I retained him discreetly to sue Atlantic College for violating my civil rights, particularly my right of free speech, by not reappointing me because I publicly opposed legalized gambling there. However, I asked the attorney, Marvin, how I could carry out my intention without involving the college dean, who had told me of my non-reappointment in confidence. Marvin and I worked out a strategy, which I then implemented.

The advisory committee for our hotel-motel management program had played a key role in the end of my career at Atlantic College, according to the dean, and I had no obligation of silence with regard to that role. Indeed, having formed the committee and treated them as my friends and associates, I felt betrayed by them and was quite angry. At their next monthly meeting, I introduced a resolution that the committee go on record as opposing casino gambling for Atlantic City because it would inevitably lead to other forms of vice, cost a great deal of money to police, and diminish the quality of life there.

I knew that the resolution would have no chance of passage, but hoped the discussion would be enlightening to the community, as all of our meetings were public, recorded so that minutes could be prepared and distributed later. The committee members were aware of that recording procedure, and indeed had sanctioned it at our first meeting, not suspecting any controversial subjects would ever arise. The recording equipment was an unobtrusive part of the audio-visual setup of the conference room in which we met at Atlantic College, and I doubted that the committee would think much about being recorded if I could get them sufficiently worked up over the resolution I was introducing. That turned out to be the case; indeed, the results were gratifying, and far more effective for my legal case than I had ever expected.

Upon reading my resolution that the committee go on record as opposing legalized gambling for Atlantic City, Tony, the chairman of the committee, got red in the face. I had distributed copies to the entire committee, wording the resolution in an inflammatory manner which I would never have done had I planned on staying at Atlantic College. I had even alluded to the area's political power structure having vested interests in getting gambling there, as I had discovered that they had been buying up land which would be sold to casino interests, mostly from Las Vegas, at vastly-inflated prices, once they got local gambling legalized. My resolution could thus potentially lose them a large fortune.

Tony's opening words were quite blunt. "What the hell is wrong with you?" he asked, but the word he used was quite a bit stronger than "hell." I smiled sweetly and told him and the committee that I could not sit by idly and allow Atlantic City to be corrupted by casinos. I began to really enjoy riling up the hotel-motel committee, knowing privately from the dean that they were behind my non-reappointment. Other members chimed in with the same lack of tact as Tony had displayed, accusing me of betraying them, of being a "Judas," and then beginning to make threats against me. The best moment came when I baited them by saying, "What are you going to do, toss me into the bay — or just get me fired from my job?" By then, Tony had lost all control, as he declared, "We'll do both!" And all of this discussion was on tape, with their prior consent. What a victory!

The meeting broke up in chaos at that point; none of the committee would even look at me. They probably realized belatedly that they had gone way too far, making recorded threats against me. But they had no access to the recording equipment, which was in a locked room, and their innate arrogance probably made them feel secure in spite of the taping. As matters developed, that security was short-lived, and I was nearly the same.

After the committee drove off in anger, I opened the audio-visual room, retrieved the tape, and immediately left the campus for Philadelphia. There, I had arranged for several copies of the tape to be made at an electronics store, one of which I put in my safe deposit box, while I mailed a second copy to a very close friend in New York with whom I had attended grade school. Peter and I had stayed in touch over the years, he had even visited me in Brigantine, and I had alerted him that a sealed package would be arriving, only to be opened if something happened to me. This was my insurance against that eventuality.

My plan was that Marvin, my attorney, would contact the president of Atlantic College discretely and inform him of my intent to sue for violation of my civil and constitutional rights. The tape established beyond a reasonable doubt (the standard of proof in such matters) that my non-reappointment was the direct result of my opposition to casino gambling in Atlantic City. Each member of the hotel-motel committee would be subpoenaed to testify under oath about their role in my non-reappointment, while the dean would be kept out of the process entirely; all he had done was to give me advance notice, while the committee and other civic leaders, and ultimately the crime syndicates, had done the dirty work.

At that point, however, matters got out of control. Little had I known that by taking on the pro-gambling interests in Atlantic City, I was also taking on those same interests in Las Vegas, and right behind them stood The Mob, the crime syndicate which had been planning for decades to bring casinos to the East. These were very serious people, and they were very unhappy with some college professor who was trying to sabotage their plans. They began to show that unhappiness even before Marvin approached the college president, as within a few days of that memorable committee meeting, I was pulled over by the Atlantic City police while my car was searched for drugs; my Cadillac convertible was torn apart, the seats ripped up, even the hubcaps removed while I had to stand by and watch the destruction. Nothing was found, but early the following morning I received an anonymous phone call, the caller stating, "Tony says hello, and wants you to know that the next time, drugs will be found, if you don't back off. This is your only warning."

After this incident, I drove to my attorney's home without even calling him first. It was Sunday morning, and he was out in his back yard gardening. I told Marvin what had just happened, expecting him to be shocked – but that was not the case. He just stared at me and told me how naïve I was, as well as shortsighted to not have anticipated something of that sort. Now I became even angrier, reminding him that he and I had cooked up the scheme of getting the committee to make damaging recorded admissions at a meeting. Marvin replied, "What I never told you to do, however, was to be so stupid. You were supposed to be discrete, to lead them along the path which would serve our purpose. It was never my intent to have you confront these hard men with your dumb anti-gambling resolution. Don't you know who these people are? They control Atlantic City, and the people behind them control Las Vegas. You are in very, very deep trouble, Eugene."

After both of us had calmed down, Marvin took me down to his basement recreation room and made some coffee while we planned strategy. It was clear that our original plan, calling for him to approach the Atlantic College president about a settlement, was now unlikely to work, as now the mob bosses were really irritated with me. We agreed that I would lay low for the remainder of the school year, while searching for another position. Marvin said that the warning call indicated that the hidden Atlantic City power structure preferred that I just make a quiet exit from the area; that was why I had been warned. It was not advantageous for them to eliminate me as there would then be an investigation. My anti-gambling position was quite well-known, I had written articles for the Atlantic City Press and other New Jersey newspapers, and so if I disappeared there would be a fuss.

It galled me to take this advice, but I did so, vowing to continue to fight casinos for Atlantic City after I had left the area. Having visited Las Vegas several times, I knew what was in store for the area if full gambling arrived: a quantum leap in drug dealing, prostitution, extortion, gambling addiction, and other forms of corruption. Vast amounts of money would be skimmed out of the new gambling industry and into the coffers of the organized crime syndicate. But, the prospect of such developments was not imminent, as legalizing casinos would require the New Jersey State Legislature's approval. I could continue to fight the casino interests once I was out of their clutches – or so I thought then. Still, I had probably succeeded in delaying the advent of casino gambling in Atlantic City, a source of great satisfaction to me. Even more satisfying was the distress I had caused the hidden mob bosses, whose front men were leading members of my hotel-motel committee at Atlantic College. So, all of the pain was not in vain!

CHAPTER SIX

◈

CAREER MOVE

While I just barely managed to complete that school year and finish my contract as professor and business division chairman at Atlantic College, events, or fate, intervened. Some days after my car had been subjected to a fake search for drugs, followed the next day by a telephone threat or warning, I was outside my house on the Brigantine shore when I heard a sharp snapping sound. I dove into the bushes in an undignified manner, which may have saved my life, as a car drove by with its lights off while there were more such sounds. The next morning, I found several obvious bullet holes in my home's wood siding. It appeared that the mob had spoken, in a most forceful manner. I was scared.

Meanwhile, I had heard about a new career opportunity which might be available. Upon taking over the business chairmanship at the College, I had also taken on several volunteer positions, not only because this was expected of college officials, but because I believed in trying to improve conditions wherever I lived. I had become a board member of the area community action agency, Atlantic Human Resources, one of the earliest agencies in the War Against Poverty which President Kennedy had proposed and President Johnson had implemented after JFK's assassination.

New Jersey and New York comprised part of Region II of OEO, the Office of Economic Opportunity, the Federal administrative arm of the War Against Poverty. Serving as a local board member, I received frequent mailings from OEO Region II, including ones containing postings of job openings throughout the Region. It seemed that the Broome County, New York, community action agency, named Opportunities for Broome, was in need of an executive director – and I was in need of a new position, and preferably not in teaching or college administration. I was ready to try something different – and I also wished to get away from the type of cowardly behavior I had experienced at Atlantic College, resulting in my losing a job for exercising my civil and constitutional rights in an effort to improve local conditions and discourage casinos.

The deadline for applications for the Broome County position was fast approaching, so I called my contacts at the Region II OEO office and inquired about it. It seemed that the previous executive director, the agency's first, had been fired on a split vote of their board, with its chairman casting the deciding vote against that previous director and then resigning himself. That description did not make the position seem very attractive – but then I considered that I had no professional experience in such agency work. I was merely a volunteer board member at Atlantic Human Resources, and therefore probably the only post I could land would be at a troubled agency such as Opportunities for Broome (the latter being the county name), which was usually shortened to just OFB.

I applied at once, first by phone to their new board chairman, a young local minister, and then by rushing an application and resume to him. Within a week, I was invited to an interview; the deadline for such interviews was fast approaching, and I would be the last candidate considered. Frankly, I did not rate my chances as very high; had I been on the OFB Board, I would not have voted to hire myself. It was a four-hour drive from my home in New Jersey to Binghamton, New York, where OFB was based, and my Board interview was scheduled for three in the afternoon the next Friday, a day on which I had no classes.

Finding that I was understandably very eager to get out of Atlantic County before the crime syndicate took even more drastic action to shut me up about casino gambling, I had decided that Atlantic College would be happy to accept my early resignation should I secure this new position. Serving as department chairman there meant that I taught only two classes each semester, both of which could be covered by other teachers if necessary. Now, the challenge was how to secure a job as head of the OFB community action agency for which I was essentially totally unqualified. My only full-time positions had been in teaching; all I had ever done in terms of the War Against Poverty was to serve on the Atlantic County agency's board. How could I maximize my slim chances?

The day before my Friday interview, I drove up to Binghamton, New York and checked into a motel along Route 7 just East of the city. At nine in the morning on Friday, I showed up at the Binghamton Public Library, and for the next four hours, I studied everything I could find out about Broome County – its history, demographics, industry, commerce, educational institutions, and particularly what Opportunities for Broome had done in the several years of its existence. All community action agencies were required to publish annual reports and other documents, all conveniently on file at the library. By one in the afternoon, I knew more about Broome County, Binghamton and the surrounding cities, the rural areas, and OFB than probably anyone on the agency board was likely to know: God bless research!

After a light lunch at a downtown Binghamton Chinese restaurant, I went to the old church where Opportunities for Broome was located and introduced myself to the staff member handling candidates. I was the only candidate left to be interviewed, and was escorted into the board meeting room in the church basement. The young minister who was serving as board chairman introduced himself, and then introduced me to the board. They had a prepared list of questions, probably originating with the Office of Economic Opportunity in New York, the funding source, which they took turns asking. Luckily for me, the first set of questions dealt with my knowledge of OEO and community action agencies, which I had gained as a board member myself in Atlantic County – rules, regulations, limitations, current developments, and so on. The next set of questions covered the history, demographics, industry, commerce, and other relevant facts about Broome County – all of the stuff which I had memorized that morning, and most of which I would forget shortly afterwards. But for the moment, I was the resident expert, answering every single question fully and correctly, and often going considerably beyond what was asked. Probably my biggest blunder was being too long-winded, a common problem with teachers.

The interview had been scheduled to take an hour, but it ran on until nearly five in the afternoon. I was then asked to leave the board room, and I went upstairs, to find that the staff had all left, as OFB closed early at four p.m. on Fridays. I waited in the OFB lobby, glancing at flyers and brochures on such programs as community organization, job training, Headstart child development, legal services, and others – but my mind was not on those materials, most of which I had seen at Atlantic Human Resources. After about half an hour, the board chairman came up the stairs from the basement board room, with a smile on his face; he was followed by most board members. "Congratulations, Eugene, you have just been appointed as our new executive director," he told me. My interview strategy had paid off; now I just had to learn how to do the job for which I was being hired. And I had better learn that job rapidly, as I was to start work at OFB in two weeks.

◇

CHAPTER SEVEN

ENDINGS

D riving back to New Jersey the next morning, I had four hours to think about my next steps. The first of those would be to give Atlantic College two weeks' notice of my leaving. Under most circumstances, such short notice to an educational institution would have been totally unacceptable, and indeed a violation of my contractual obligations. In this unique case, however, I knew that the Dean and College President would breathe a sigh of relief that I was leaving, as they had received their marching orders from the hidden power structure in Atlantic County, just as I had received threats and then gunshots to get me out of the way. The first round of those gunshots had missed on purpose; I was certain that if a second round occurred, it would turn out to be my last day on earth.

The President of Atlantic College happened to also live on Brigantine, where I lived; indeed, he had a mansion in the central part of that Island. I arrived there around noon the day after my interview, having left early the next morning and thanks to the relatively light traffic around New York City on weekend mornings. I took a chance and stopped by the elegant home of the President, and rang the doorbell without calling first, as I had a bone to pick with him, feeling that he was the culprit who had turned my contract non-renewal over to the Dean. Our then-President was not a man of courage; in fact, his unkind nickname was "Jellylegs," emanating from his refusal to back faculty raises the previous year because the State Board of Higher Education opposed them. He had also refused to renew the contract of my friend, the former biology department chairman, due to the latter´s civil rights activities. The man did not deserve respect, nor did he have it.

Jellylegs answered his doorbell, and was obviously displeased to see me. He was a short man with wavy hair and a cultivated British accent, which was an affectation. I told him that I had urgent business and asked for an audience, which he reluctantly granted. We sat down in his study; no refreshments were offered, and there was no welcome. I could not tell him that the Dean had tipped his hand and told me I would not be allowed to continue as business department chairman; so I had arranged an alternative story, one which was quite true, but also purposely incomplete in that the Dean's role was omitted.

First, I informed the President of my earlier fake motor vehicle violation; the warning a police sergeant had given me on the spot that if I continued to be a troublemaker, the next time I would suffer far worse consequences; then followed by the anti-gambling resolution I had introduced to my hotel-motel advisory committee; the blowup by Tony, the committee chair, and other members; and finally, the gunshots fired at me outside my house a few evenings later. I embellished a bit, adding some threatening phone calls when there had actually been only one such call. I was watching the President closely; he had an expressive face but he displayed no surprise at any of this. Rather, he was stone-faced and obviously unmoved by my recitation.

Then, my subdued anger came to the surface. Having been threatened and shot at, all for an act of conscience, namely my opposition to legalized gambling for Atlantic City, I had become very frustrated at having little recourse. Therefore, without even pausing for breath, I told the President that I could not in good conscience remain at Atlantic College any longer, as my civil and constitutional rights were being violated; and further I knew very well that he was part of the power structure and would never defend me in any way. I reminded him of how he had failed to champion his own faculty and staff for justified pay raises, and I further told him that nobody at the college had much respect for him.

I awaited his reaction to my outburst. The night before, after my successful interview at Opportunities for Broome, I had done a handwritten letter of resignation from Atlantic College, on a yellow legal pad I had brought for notes during my trip to Binghamton. That letter gave Atlantic College two weeks' notice that I was leaving my post, due to what appeared to be the College's complicity in the abuse of my rights. I cited the hotel-motel committee's threatening comments after I had introduced a resolution opposing casino gambling; since it was an official college committee, its misconduct could be construed as also that of the College. Of course, I did not mention that I had baited that committee into its attack on me. Instead, I cited ongoing fears for my safety should I remain in Atlantic County.

Jellylegs surprised me at that point. He pondered my words for a minute, and then said, "Eugene, you are making a wise move. Had you not taken this initiative, we would have acted – and your present contract would be your last one at Atlantic College. You may be surprised at my reaction supporting your decision, but you are well liked and well respected at the college. You were chosen Teacher of the Year last year for that reason. Of course, I cannot comment on any of your allegations, which may well end up in court. But I do hereby accept your resignation, even on only two weeks' notice. We can handle your administrative duties for the rest of the year, and your classes can be taught by others. I wish you good luck and Godspeed." With those words, I was free of my job, and was soon to be free of Atlantic County, New Jersey.

The next day was Monday, and I called several moving companies as OFB, my new employer, had agreed to pay in full for the move, per government guidelines. I began packing up immediately, only taking time off to teach my two classes. I said goodbye to friends and colleagues, giving them a truncated and sanitized version of the situation. My public opposition to legalized gambling in the area was well known, as it had been the subject of several newspaper articles and op-ed pieces. I had no reason to hide the threats and other incidents which had occurred, although I feared I might appear cowardly to some people. But that seemed not to be the case; there was not a single individual at the college or elsewhere who blamed me for leaving rather suddenly. It was gratifying that one friend, a leader of the Black community, even commended my efforts on their behalf.

My next-door neighbor in Brigantine perhaps said what others were thinking. Bill was a retired Philadelphia business executive who had moved, with his wife, into his former summer home and converted it into a lovely year-round house on the Inland Waterway. We had become friendly, since we both had warm feelings towards Philadelphia, where he had built a successful career while I had attended graduate school at the University of Pennsylvania there. Bill was also a loyal Penn alumni and we had even attended college football games together.

Bill and his wife invited me for a final dinner shortly before I left permanently for OFB and Binghamton, New York. After dinner, Bill and I had brandy and good cigars in his recreation room; I suspected the cigars were Cuban, smuggled through the blockade. He leaned back in his reclining chair and said, "Eugene, you are lucky to get away while the getting is good. I know some of the people whom you have offended by opposing casinos for Atlantic City. Most of them come from the Philadelphia mob, and I hated paying protection money to them so that my business would not be burned down. They are very determined people, with much to lose if casinos do not come here, and I thought about warning you when you began to publicly oppose gambling interests. I heard the gunshots the night you had to dive into your bushes to avoid being shot – and, believe me, if they wanted you dead then, we would not be having this conversation now. Get out while you still can; there will be no second chances."

CHAPTER EIGHT

◆

CLIFFHANGER

It seemed that my feet were firmly set on a new path, or even several new paths at once. But there were to be some stumbles along the way. While I was preparing for a speedy move to Binghamton, New York, to assume my new position as executive director at Opportunities for Broome – my first full-time job outside of college and university teaching – the pro-gambling interests in Atlantic City had decided that I was not to be allowed to leave smoothly. Perhaps that was ironic, since they wanted me gone badly enough to arrange for non-renewal of my college contract, a fake car drug search, threats, and even gunshots. But probably they saw teachers at Atlantic College as a potential threat, and wanted to insure that no other faculty or staff continued my efforts to oppose casinos for the area. That would also explain why my wrongful non-renewal was leaked.

I found out about the new form of their pressure on me a few days later, just as I was completing preparations for the move to New York State. About ten one night, my phone rang, and the young minister chairing the OFB Board was on the other end. He asked me if I had heard from the Binghamton newspapers (there were two then, the Press and the Sun Bulletin). I had not heard from them, and told him so. He then told me that there had been an anonymous phone call to the most popular radio talk show host, taken on the air, where the caller told the host – and his entire Broome County audience – that the new OFB executive director had been fired down in Atlantic County, New Jersey, for being a "major troublemaker" as well as other unspecified offenses. OFB wanted the full and true story at once and before confirming my appointment as agency executive director.

It did not take me long to decide what to do; I stated that I would like to come up for a special meeting of the Opportunities for Broome Board of Directors, with the press invited, including that radio talk show host. I asked for the opportunity to make the full situation clear, as while I had alluded to my desire to leave teaching for the "real world" of community action when I was interviewed for the job, I had not gotten into any other reasons for wanting to leave my position and Atlantic County. I had felt that they were private – but now those private reasons had been made public in a very distorted fashion.

The Board chairman agreed at once, stating that this would clear the air and allow the Board to ask any questions it wished about the entire situation. Since the Bylaws required three days' notice of any special board meeting, and the next day was a Friday, the meeting was called for the following Monday evening. Now, I had to decide whether to put my move on hold until this snag was resolved, one way or the other. While I had done nothing wrong, I had learned as a board member myself at the Atlantic County community action agency that such agencies detested unnecessary controversy. It was ironic, as they were chartered to change the then-reactionary social and human services system – but when it came to bad publicity, they could be very conservative. The odds for my survival as their new executive director were therefore not very good, unless I was totally truthful and totally convincing.

In planning for this special board meeting, I first decided that I needed "backup" to come with me, and the next day I called the Minister back and he agreed to let me bring one or two people as witnesses and to vouch for my character. I chose the former head of the College's Biology Department, who had lost his position the year before for taking on the Atlantic City power structure over the exploitation and rampant poverty there. Chuck immediately agreed to come up to Binghamton on short notice and to tell his own story, as well as vouching for mine, as he was a native of the area who had advised me informally as to how to oppose legalized gambling most effectively. Of course, in retrospect, he might have warned me that I was jeopardizing my job, just as Chuck had jeopardized, and lost, his own position – but had he done so, I probably would not have listened. In my naivete, I had felt invulnerable.

As to the other person to help plead my cause, I chose the president of the local League of Women Voters, whose credentials went back to the Daughters of the American Revolution. She was the perfect matron, of impeccable reputation, not a "troublemaker," but I knew that Bernice hated legalized gambling, believing it would ruin what was left of the charm and verve of Atlantic City. On Monday morning, the three of us started the long drive to OFB, stopping only for dinner at a diner along the way. I had plenty of time to provide them with the complete background on the situation.

I had planned our arrival for a half hour before the special board meeting at 8:00 p.m. That way, I was able to introduce my two witnesses as the Board arrived. The Chairman convened the meeting promptly; the board had thirty-one members including its chair, and each and every one was present. There were also reporters from both Binghamton newspapers, the radio talk show host, and camera crews from both television stations. It was only later that I learned that Arlene, our official staff member from Region II of the Federal Office of Economic Opportunity, and a staffer from the New York Governor's Office, were also present. Apparently, my appointment had become a big deal.

The Board Chairman opened the meeting by saying merely that the special meeting had been called to discuss whether any facts, rumors, or allegations had come to light which might cast doubt on my appointment as OFB's executive head. He did not cite the allegations, as they were well known; and I learned later that a transcript of the radio talk show segment dealing with them had been sent out with the call for the Board meeting.

At that point the meeting was turned over to me for my explanations, and I then introduced the two people who had accompanied me, giving a brief biography of each. Chuck began his presentation, first explaining how he had lost his job as chairman of the Atlantic College biology department for championing the cause of minorities and the poor in Atlantic City, where they were exploited, abused, and even killed for objecting to the deplorable conditions there. He concluded his remarks by saying, "Yes, Eugene is a troublemaker; and if I were a betting man, I would have bet that he would not have been reappointed next year, suffering my fate. But he is also an honorable man who has the courage of his convictions. He does not give in, and he does not give up. If that is the kind of person you want as your next executive director, then he deserves the job. You and the community here will be well-served, and he will never disappoint you."

Bernice, the head of the area League of Women Voters, spoke next. I had first met her when we both served on the board of Atlantic Human Resources, that area's community action agency, which was comparable to OFB. We had worked on other projects as well, and she was totally opposed to allowing casinos in Atlantic City (a fight she eventually lost, unfortunately). She began her remarks with some facts about herself which I had not known; she too had been harassed, threatened, and put at risk due to her activist role in the community and against its power structure. Her husband had lost his local job and now commuted to Philadelphia. She knew just what had been done to me; I had been given "the unfair Atlantic County treatment" – but I was totally blameless. By the time Bernice had finished her remarks, I found that I was choked up.

The Chairman then offered the Board the opportunity to ask questions of me or either of the two previous speakers. I waited expectantly, when I saw one Board Member ask to speak. It was a leading local attorney who had been on the OFB Board since its inception several years before, also serving as its former chairman. He said, "Mr. Chairman, I move the confirmation of the appointment of our new executive director." While I was surprised at that move, I was even more surprised by another voice, a woman from Binghamton Social Services, who said, "I second Ted's motion and call the question."

This parliamentary procedure meant that there would first be a vote on calling the question, and should that vote pass, there could be no further discussion; the motion to confirm my appointment would be voted up or down, as the case might be. I tried to appear calm, but was in fact extremely nervous, as my future at OFB clearly hung in the balance. It required a two-thirds vote to call the question, and the result went quite a bit beyond that; the vote was, in fact, unanimous. But I was still nervous, as it could be that the lawyer's original motion would be voted down, leaving me between a rock and a hard place, and out of a job.

The OFB chairman then said that he would ask for a roll-call vote, for the record, so that there would never be any issue with its outcome, such as might occur with a simple showing of hands. The Board Secretary, a large woman representing the low-income residents of Broome County, called out the names of each Board member – and each and every one voted **yes,** to confirm my appointment unanimously. I had not said a word at the meeting, except for introducing my two guests and supporters. Still, I was now confirmed as the new executive director of the Opportunities for Broome agency. It was a memorable outcome; I was very grateful, and said a silent prayer of thanks.

I had traded my dear old Cadillac convertible on a used Chrysler Imperial, an elegant and large car befitting, I thought, the head of a community action agency who often had to transport people. I would have felt that it was a bit showy, but in those days of cheap gasoline and large families, big cars and trucks were favored. Also, the Chrysler was a few years old, which took away some of its ostentation (although the Broome County news media never tired of mentioning it). Chuck and Bernice fell asleep in the car on the way home; it had been a very long drive, a very tiring day, and we were all exhausted. I pulled into a rest area on the Garden State Parkway, more than halfway to Brigantine, to take a nap; I could drive no further without rest, nor could either of my passengers.

I had trouble falling asleep, however, as my mind was in a turmoil – and not just over my new position, the details of the move, and the leave taking from Atlantic County. My life was changing in more ways than one, and I began to wonder whether I could handle so many new challenges. Just before finally falling asleep in the car, I recalled a sign I had seen in the reception room at the Israeli Consulate in New York. The sign quoted a founder of the State of Israel; I was not sure which one, but I remembered the quote; "If you will it, it is not a dream." Whatever was happening or going to happen to me, it would not be a dream; it would become my new reality. Content, I finally fell into slumber.

CHAPTER NINE

◆

DEADLINE

Upon reaching Atlantic County once more, and just before dropping them off at their homes, I thanked my two friends-and-supporters profusely. I had not really known what they would say; indeed, it might even have worked against my chances for the position. Nor had I been sure that they were the best people to plead my case; I had thought about asking the executive director of Atlantic Human Resources to come to OFB with me. But then I considered that the OFB board might feel that, as a member of AHR's own board, I had pressured him to testify on my behalf, which would certainly work against me. At the root of my job problem were matters of trust and of honor. Chuck and Bernice were the two people in Atlantic County in whom I had the most trust, and whom I considered the most honorable. Ultimately, those were the reasons for my choosing them.

Other than teaching my classes at Atlantic College, the remainder of my time in New Jersey was spent getting ready to move to Broome County, New York. I had rented a small temporary apartment in Binghamton, within walking distance of Opportunities for Broome, so that I could take my time finding a more permanent residence. My furniture, household goods, and similar items were all packed and the mover had a key to my NJ house, so as to be able to load up all of my goods. I had decided to keep the actual moving date flexible until I found a home. Being an inveterate collector, my most-prized items were carefully packed in my Imperial; that was one reason I had chosen such a large car. Friends joked that its trunk could hold a couple of bodies – a joke which I did not find terribly funny, after being the target of gunshots in my own Brigantine yard.

The next few weeks were intensely busy. I found that serving as a board member at Atlantic Human Resources provided very little preparation for running my own agency. Board members were fed a diet of accomplishments and other positives; the staff of such agencies kept the problems to themselves, at least until on occasion those problems came to board or public attention. At Opportunities for Broome, the similar pattern had been for any issues to be handled quietly, or unfortunately not handled at all.

After about two weeks at my new job, I received a call from the Office of Economic Opportunity, our major funding source, which had been established by legislation first proposed by President Kennedy and then implemented by President Lyndon Johnson after JFK's tragic assassination. That legislation established the War on Poverty, a major Federal initiative, and divided the nation into ten regional OEO supervisory offices. Region II was headquartered in downtown New York City, with Milt as regional director. I had never spoken with Milt, but Arlene, OFB's field representative from OEO, had attended the meeting at which my appointment was confirmed, and had welcomed me to the program. Understandably, nothing had come up then regarding OFB.

Therefore, I was surprised when Milt himself called me, shortly after I began working in Binghamton, and instinctively I closed my office door to listen to him. He began by asking me if I knew about OFB's past problems, and I indicated that naturally I had studied my new agency's history and had tried to draw out more information from key staff at our weekly meetings, but they had been vague. Milt said he was not surprised, as the OFB staff had been hiding the likely defunding and termination of the agency due to its fiscal blunders and other serious issues; I was in charge of a "very troubled agency."

It seemed that Opportunities for Broome, like many community action agencies, had attracted well-meaning but often incompetent staff

– do-gooders who did not know how to do good efficiently and consistently, in compliance with Federal rules and guidelines. The boards of such agencies were usually inexperienced themselves, dominated by representatives of the populations served by the agency, and often incapable of making wise decisions. It seemed that "the blind were leading the blind", a politically-incorrect expression one could still use in those days. Milt then asked me to come to the New York City OEO office within the next few days, as he had obtained a temporary extension of OFB's funding from Washington, on the strength of the agency's having a new executive director who supposedly would be able to handle fiscal and program matters, having taught about them for years at several colleges. We were being given one last chance, but the cards were clearly stacked against us, short of some miracle which I felt quite unlikely to be able to pull off.

Taking the bull by the horns, I told Milt I would be in his office at one in the afternoon the next day, since it would take over three hours to drive down from Binghamton to New York City. I immediately had a memo sent out to all key staff, including about a dozen program directors, convening an urgent meeting for eight the following morning. Some of them had developed a tendency to drift in around an hour later than that, a practice I had already changed by having a timed sign-up sheet for all incoming staff. As to the agenda for that emergency staff meeting, I used only two words: OEO ISSUES. I was sure that would be sufficient to generate everyone's attendance, and I was right.

We met around the conference table in my office, with the door closed and orders that we were not to be disturbed. I realized this would generate all sorts of nervous rumors; that was part of my intent. We were going to get to the bottom of OFB/OEO problems. Calling the meeting to order, I reported on my call the previous day from the OEO regional director, and then told the key staff that I would be leaving for New York City as soon as this meeting was over, and that it had better produce a full explanation of the agency's problems.

There was total silence for a minute, then replaced by a babble of voices. From what I could decipher, everyone was disclaiming knowledge that we had any problems. I had anticipated that happening, as frankly I did not have a terribly high regard for this group. Therefore, I had already reviewed the agency records stored in the basement, containing many memos and other communications from OEO complaining about OFB's problems. Overriding the babblers, I began to read from the memos; even if my voice carried out through the closed office door, we did not open officially for another half hour, and our staff were not noted for coming in early.

The babble, however, turned out not to be a problem, as when I read from the most critical memo first, there was sudden silence, allowing me to lower my voice. That memo had been issued when the previous executive director lost his job, as he had gone down to OEO on his own afterwards and had met with the Regional Director to confirm that the agency was not able to follow many federal guidelines. He claimed that he had been the sacrificial lamb as the staff had bad-mouthed him to the OFB Board of Directors to put all of the blame on him, not on other senior staff. It seemed that that little secret had been hidden from me when I had first been interviewed. It seemed that there had been little disclosure of known agency issues during my initial interview, or afterwards!

This OEO memo had been sent to the former Board Chairman, who had then resigned when the former executive director, a friend of his, was fired. The memo came into the agency, addressed to that former chairman, who was still listed as the key OFB official in OEO's records. Instead of forwarding that major memo to the new chairman, senior staff had read the memo, and then hidden it. I had only been able to find it because Milt had referred to it, and searching late the previous night I found it stuffed into the bottom drawer of the planning director's desk (my nickname for him was Dave the Dumb).

OFB had been given one month to get its house in order, and more than half of that month was already gone. I asked the staff what they had planned on doing when the remainder of OFB's short lease-on-life expired; there was total silence. Then I asked them pointedly to raise their hands if their resumes were already out on the street, being circulated now to other agencies, as I believed that some disloyal OFB staff behaved just like rats deserting a sinking ship.

Naturally, no hands were raised, but my point had been well made. I then told the staff that I needed to leave for New York City "to try to buy some time to clean up the horrid mess created by their incompetence, malfeasance, and just plain stupidity." They were all put on probation on the spot, and evaluations of each and every senior staff member would be done within a week, presented to each person for comments, and then, as I put it, "further decisions would be made." I pretended to be totally calm, and cold as ice, as I had never had any similar problems with the teachers of the two college business divisions I had headed. Inside, though, I was seething – but that alone would not remove our impending doom. The important thing was to force major changes for the better by the agency's key staff. I then demanded another meeting at eight the following morning, with written and verbal reports to be presented by each division head as to our priorities: what needed to be corrected at once, along with a time frame for further vital changes. As I left then for my meeting with Milt at OEO, I felt that we were at least on the upward path. The journey of a thousand miles is said to begin with a single step, and we had at least taken that first step. But, would the remainder of those essential steps follow soon enough to save OFB? The jury was indeed out on that major question; time would tell.

CHAPTER TEN

◆

ASSIGNMENTS

The emergency key staff meeting at OFB had taken longer than I had expected; and I had to speed down Route 7 and then the parkways leading into New York City to meet with Milt, the regional head of OEO. Luckily, traffic was fairly light along the way, and I arrived on time and was ushered into Milt's office. I saw that OEO field representative Arlene was also present, along with Angel, the deputy regional director. The three of them reminded me of the "hanging judges" in the Old Wild West – except that in this case, it was our agency whose existence was at stake.

Milt opened the meeting with some general comments about how troubled OFB was, how long those troubles had existed, how patient OEO had been with OFB, and so on. He then turned to Arlene to fill in the details, which she did with gusto. While she was more supportive than the other two present at the meeting, she had her responsibilities. When things went wrong at one of the agencies which she monitored, it might be blamed on her by OEO, so she could not pull too many punches. I listened to the recitation in silence; much of it I had discovered for myself, but there were some new items raised. Milt concluded by saying that I was being informed that the agency was going to be defunded; the issue was more one of just when that would occur, rather than if it would happen. (I later learned that OFB's funding had already been promised elsewhere.)

Now, it was my turn. I had read the Federal regulations and Office of Economic Opportunity guidelines regarding such defunding actions carefully over lunch on the way down to New York City. Rather than trying to deny or challenge any of the assertions made by Milt and Arlene, which would have been foolish since I was clearly a newcomer without first-hand knowledge, I simply told them fully about the morning's emergency key staff meeting and that I was determined to get to the bottom of all of the problems, and then resolve them at once. Further, I pointed out that the law establishing OEO gave any agency in trouble a thirty-day grace period to attempt to correct the situation to OEO's satisfaction. I invited all three of the OEO officials then present to come to a meeting in Binghamton in thirty days' time, to review our progress and ask any questions which they wished. My proposal was fully discussed and critiqued – but since the law provided this remedy, it had to be accepted by the OEO Region II staff, as I had truly hoped.

Satisfied with the outcome of the meeting, I walked around New York City for a while. Then I drove across the Queensboro Bridge to visit my mother Anne at her old Rego Park apartment, and we had dinner at a nearby Sizzler steak restaurant. While I had succeeded in saving OFB from immediate defunding, my agency's future was far from assured. So, I told mother that the meeting had just been routine, while wishing that had been the case.

CHAPTER ELEVEN

◈

BROOME COUNTY

It took a great deal of coffee to get me ready for the next morning's staff meeting. Trying my best to appear bright-eyed and confident, I explained to the staff that we had been given a thirty-day funding extension by the Office of Economic Opportunity, as provided by law and by my persuasiveness. Then each senior staff member presented his or her report, read aloud while copies were circulated to the entire group. The staff then "brainstormed" each report, critiquing it and making further suggestions. They were a bright group of people, and many useful ideas emerged which nobody had thought of previously. My former academic background was very useful, as this type of process had become quite standard in management situations about which I taught, but was not common then at community agencies such as OFB – so I was moderately encouraged.

This second part of our meeting took most of the day; we sent out for sandwiches for lunch, and by the end of the day a Master Plan had emerged which would begin being implemented at once. Over the next two weeks, I evaluated each senior staff member, while each of them in turn evaluated his or her own staff. Several people were told to leave, and I took on the responsibility for making those ultimate decisions so as to avoid any cronyism or other suspicions of favoritism or grudges. Being new myself, I had no ties to anyone or to any department, and thus could do my best to decide employees' fates based on the merits.

By the final week before the scheduled visit from the top Region II OEO officials, our Master Plan was in place, implementation had begun, and thus that last week was spent preparing reports to be presented to our Board of Directors as well as to the OEO representatives. The news media had, of course, gotten wind of the agency's problems; I later learned that we had several "moles" on both the staff and the Board who leaked OFB news at will. Since Board meetings were required to be public, we called that special session a meeting of the Committee of the Whole, a parliamentary trick which allowed us to keep the meeting closed and private.

Later, I learned that Milt, Arlene, and Angel, the OEO officials, had already decided that our agency would be defunded immediately after this meeting, and that they only came up to our special session because it was required by the legislation. However, and contrary to their intent, they were so impressed with the reports presented at the meeting, the progress we were making, the support of our Board, and our plans for the future, that we were re-funded for the following year. If we justified their faith, we would return to good standing as an OEO community action agency. I was informed of that outcome the following day by a call from Region II OEO in New York City. All of us, staff and Board, could breathe a sigh of relief; the only disappointed group was the news media, who had been hoping to see our agency blood spilled because that would make a better news story. It seemed that bad news was preferable to good news, seeming to be a fairly universal rule of journalism.

With our funding assured, at least for the time being, and solid plans in place for the immediate future of Opportunities for Broome, I was able to focus on other matters. The most urgent of these was locating a suitable house, as I had been temporarily living in a small apartment in Binghamton, with my goods and furniture mostly still stored in New Jersey. So, each weekend and some evenings, I began to tour Broome County to see what was available, with several realtors helping me since I did not yet know the area.

Since my agency was charged with fighting both urban and rural poverty, and Broome County was primarily rural outside of the cities of Binghamton, Endicott, Johnson City, and Vestal, my house-hunting focused primarily on some small towns and villages in the outlying area. One Sunday, I was heading South on Route 7 after checking out housing in the famous village of Sanitaria Springs, once a major resort for people needing natural hot springs for health reasons. As I continued down the road towards the next town, I saw a sign for a place simply called Tunnel, with a small side road to the left. That place name intrigued me, and I traveled a few miles up the side road to find a tiny village with a broken-down former cheese factory, a one-room post office, and little else. As I crossed a railroad track just beyond the post office, there on my left was a very old house with a For Sale sign outside, so I decided to check it out.

Within a month, I had become the new owner of that large old house, its several acres of land, and its long history. There had been a battle between two rival railroad gangs in Tunnel in the mid-Nineteenth Century, and the wounded had been taken to my "old new home." The house was a two-story frame with ugly gray siding, heated in part by a gigantic coal stove which also provided cooking surfaces, and with eight rooms plus a large dirt-floored basement and an attic. It had the classic Upstate New York front porch with pillars. The house used a spring for water, which clogged at times and dried up in late summer. It was run down, but as executive director of the area anti-poverty agency, I felt that it was perfectly suitable, making the statement that rural poverty was a reality in Broome County.

Over the next month, I had my furniture and other items moved up from New Jersey. That allowed me to make a trip back to Atlantic County, to also see how my lawsuit against Atlantic College was coming; I had sued the institution for violating my civil and constitutional rights by not renewing my contract, admittedly because I had taken a stand against legalized gambling for Atlantic City. My lawyer felt that the College would want to settle out-of-court to avoid adverse publicity, particularly given the role of the crime syndicate in causing me to lose my job.

It turned out that my lawyer was quite correct; the College had made an offer to him which would cover the cost of the house I was buying in Tunnel, New York, so that I could cancel the mortgage which I had just taken out (luckily, there was no prepayment penalty). After negotiating a bit through my lawyer, the College upped its proposal, and I accepted that increased offer. One factor encouraging my acceptance was that I did not feel safe in Atlantic County, and had neither the time nor the desire to participate in an extended lawsuit. At some point, I was sure that the crime syndicate would decide that just getting rid of me would put an end to a trial's publicity against legalizing gambling there. I had escaped their retribution once, and had no desire to test them a second time.

CHAPTER TWELVE

◆

"COUNTRY SQUIRE"

And so life settled down to what passes for normal in Broome County, New York. Before the brutal upstate New York winter settled in, I had moved my stuff from New Jersey, and myself from the small apartment in Binghamton. I was now a resident of Tunnel, New York, one of some twenty-nine families residing there at the time. Just across Tunnel Road, as I had discovered that little back road off Route 7 was named, the Millers were my nearest neighbors: middle-aged husband and wife, two kids, along with Josephine and Snooper. Josephine was the oldest dog recorded in Broome County, an Airedale, who had achieved a near-miraculous twenty-eight years and now mostly lay around on the couch. Snooper, on the other hand, was a Basset Hound who loved to roam and had taken over my living room. Now, Snooper was challenged for turf rights by my own dog, Springer, a mostly-Springer Spaniel who had been around for nearly ten years by then. He had been found on the streets of Dayton, Ohio, by my father, remaining with my mother and me after my father died. New Jersey friends had kept him until I was settled in my new location, as dogs were not allowed in my apartment in Binghamton. Now, having moved to Tunnel, I was happy to reclaim Springer.

The situation at Opportunities for Broome improved with the implementation of our new Master Plan, which allowed for me to participate in OEO regional activities. The executive directors of all of the community action agencies in Region II, which included New York State, met monthly at the Office of Economic Opportunity in New York City.

Those meetings allowed me to visit with my mother Anne in Rego Park, Queens, across the East River from the Lower Manhattan OEO offices. We had our choice of restaurants near her apartment, and I usually chose a popular Chinese place with many options.

Binghamton, New York, was the home base of State Senator Warren Anderson, a very powerful official, and my agency was involved with our Congressman and U.S. Senators as well. Thus, we began to lobby informally for their support for the War Against Poverty. While most public officials deplored the plight of the poor, disadvantaged, and of some minorities, there was great controversy over using Federal and State funds to help them. The tactic of having delegations from the groups which we served meet with these elected officials produced at least expressions of support for continued agency funding. On occasion, we even had busloads of local people travel to Washington, an overnight trip, to demonstrate responsibly and encourage Congress to meet the needs of our people. These efforts intensified as we had to compete with many other priorities.

Meanwhile, I found that there were several things I was missing in Broome County: one was the academic life. Since my previous career had been in higher education, I decided to find a part-time academic post while working at OFB. Applying to the Binghamton campus of the State University of New York, called SUNY-B locally, I offered to teach a practicum in the War Against Poverty, including classroom work and hands-on internships at my agency. The SUNY-B curriculum committee approved the proposal, and that next spring semester, I renewed my teaching career, working with several co-instructors since this practicum was an interdisciplinary program.

An unexpected result of the practicum came from the placement of one Manpower (as the program was then called) trainee in the laboratory of a senior SUNY-B chemistry professor. Our trainee was testing food products for heavy metal contamination, and found that tuna fish contained concentrations of deadly mercury compounds. While the senior chemistry prof took credit for the discovery, OFB was noted by OEO as actually initiating this major accomplishment; we were thus back in OEO's good graces by then!

CHAPTER THIRTEEN

◈

ECCLESIASTES

As time went by, the War against Poverty continued to decline into a mock-battle. What President Kennedy had envisioned as a permanent cure for one of the major evils of America, and what President Johnson had seen enacted into law by Congress, was eroded into a minimally-funded effort to provide services to rather limited groups of low-and-moderate-income Americans. There were several reasons for the decline of the historic anti-poverty program: the increased demands of our other War, the one in Vietnam; the resistance of reactionary forces in the U.S. who desperately feared an empowered low-income sector; and the growth of resistance from the so-called conservatives, who felt threatened by the rise in the power of minority groups. What had begun as a noble and innovative experimental program was declining into just one more stale and trite way of keeping the poor quiet. America had lost the War Against Poverty, and more and more of its "soldiers and officers" had surrendered, often to unemployment and even despair.

At my agency, Opportunities for Broome, some special problems had emerged which compounded the general malaise of the anti-poverty program. Our Board structure had been changed, with my wrongheaded but enthusiastic support, so that the majority of the board now came from the poor sector itself. This was an option under the legislation, and was seen as a form of self-determination for those served by the program, which is why I supported the change – a change which ironically led to my undoing as OFB's top leader.

Matters came to a head when a group of Board members and staff attended a regional conference in Buffalo, New York. The chairwoman of the Board had driven up to the meeting, but had transmission trouble on the way home. The next week, she came into my office and presented a large bill for the replacement of the transmission in her elderly Continental automobile. I told her that we could not pay the bill, as her transmission had been on its way out for a long time, and the conference trip was just its last gasp; Federal guidelines allowed for a healthy mileage allowance for Board travel, but that was all. I was perhaps not at my most tactful, as I had been alerted that several of my staff had told her that we would pay for her transmission, and I then had to deliver the bad news to her.

Within the month, a notice was posted at our office calling an Emergency Board Meeting, which could be called by as few as three Board members; not surprisingly, the Board Chair and two of her friends called the meeting, demanding that it be closed in order to discuss unspecified "personnel matters". Having received only very positive evaluations from the Board's Personnel Committee, I had no inkling that my position was the "personnel matter" under discussion, but still I was very puzzled by this unusual step. It did not take me long to find out the truth, as several friendly Board members called me that same morning to tell me that my tenure at Opportunities for Broome was being challenged because I had refused to authorize payment of that improper auto repair bill.

That evening, I began to consider leaving my job, not only because of the unpleasant upcoming emergency Board meeting from which I would be excluded – but also because of the decline and impending demise of the War Against Poverty itself. I consulted the attorney who was a former OFB Board Chairman, and who advised me to leave quietly. The former director had indeed been put through a similar removal process, had fought for his job and lost it. That was sound advice; but instead, I decided to fight for my job.

There is little point to detailing the intense struggle which followed, with both Board and staff members choosing sides for the battle. It was not long until the news media, particularly the two Binghamton newspapers, were tipped off and were waiting outside that emergency Board meeting for any tidbits of information they could secure. The morning after that meeting, their headlines stated that I was in the "fight of my life" to keep my job as Executive Director of OFB. Little did they know that, compared to my earlier fight with the organized crime forces in Atlantic City over legalizing gambling there, this latest fight seemed rather tame.

It did not remain tame, however. The Board members supporting me began to receive anonymous threats, and some of them suddenly lost various Federal and State benefits which they had been legally and properly receiving. One Board member turned out to lack legal residency status in the United States, and was threatened with deportation. It was clear that my staff, still stinging from the unfavorable evaluations I had given some of them when we were nearly defunded, had now found a golden retaliatory opportunity. They had been storing up little tidbits of "information" which they now used to what they saw as their advantage, not only against me but, far worse, against my supporters on the Board. It was those latter actions against innocent parties which were truly despicable.

The Emergency Board Meeting had placed an item on the next regular Board Meeting agenda, with the title: Status of the Executive Director. The handwriting was clearly on the wall, and during the three weeks until that next meeting, I considered various actions, either in the Broome County area or beyond it. I could fight to the last breath for my position, or I could yield. What finally decided me, though, was what was being done to the loyal Board members by those who had power over them in one form or another. None of them complained to me, but it would have been grossly unfair for them to become pawns or casualties in my battle. Further, it was clear that the days of the War Against Poverty were numbered, and within a couple of years agencies such as Opportunities for Broome would become mere providers of services to the poor and minorities. One of America's most noble experiments was winding down, and there was little to be gained by fighting over its remaining crumbs.

Accordingly, I determined upon a dramatic strategy for the next Board meeting. Before the Board chair could introduce the first agenda item on the status of the executive director, I rose to the floor and said, "Madame chairwoman, I call a point of order." I was the only staff member allowed to do this, and was also the Board parliamentarian. When asked about my point of order, I stated, "The first agenda item is now irrelevant, as I have resigned my position as your Executive Director as of the time of this meeting. Here is my letter of resignation." which I then handed to the entire Board as well as to the news media present. In that letter, I did not pull any punches; I outlined the exact and full history which had led to this moment, the complicity of key staff in the matter, the pressure tactics used against Board members who refused to participate in the plot, and my resulting unwillingness to be a party to such wrongful shenanigans. I closed the letter of resignation with the following statement, which I read then: "Ecclesiastes says that there is a time for all things, a time to sow and a time to reap, a time to keep and a time to lose, a time to fight and a time to refrain. This is my time to refrain from the fight. I much prefer to leave this agency intact, and with my best wishes for its future."

CHAPTER FOURTEEN

◆

OPPORTUNITY

Although my speech was bold, there was not a great deal of confidence underlying it. Never before had I left one job without having another already in hand. Now, for the first time, unless I found another suitable position in Broome County, I would be leaving the area, including my historic home in the Town of Tunnel, New York. I was very nervous.

Still, I had decided to be at my OFB office very promptly the next morning, as I was absolutely determined to appear in control of the situation, and to be truly professional – even in the face of the embarrassing fact that I would soon be part of OFB history.

I had already decided that I would first try to return to teaching, at least for the immediate future. The War Against Poverty was on the way out, so another community action agency job would not be advisable. Further, after all of the publicity over my situation at OFB, it was unlikely that I would be offered a comparable position at any other agency in Broome County. Social agencies are notoriously conservative, which is perhaps ironic given their mission of changing things for the better for their clients. It was also the reality that I was unlikely to find a full-time job at SUNY-Binghamton, even though I had taught a practicum there. My connection with that institution resulted solely from my position at OFB; when that position ended, so would my SUNY-Binghamton connection. Universities were just as conservative as social agencies, perhaps even more so.

Therefore, I determined to call the faculty placement firm which I had used once before, when I had left Antioch for Atlantic College. They were a national agency, and although my timing was less than ideal (being in the middle of a semester), at least I knew they would do their best for me as a former client.

As the next several weeks passed, however, I became increasingly concerned about securing a job. Still, the enjoyable part of that period was striding proudly into my office at OFB while some key staff averted their gazes, trying to pretend I no longer existed. It was thus that I learned which staff members had conspired with the Board president to get rid of me. I had determined upon a scheme which might be called payback, a nicer term than revenge. In my concluding days at OFB, I wrote glowing recommendations for each and every staffer whom I believed had betrayed me – knowing that my own good recommendation would make life most difficult for that staff member, now that the Board had taken over control of OFB. One in particular, the Planning Director, I recommended to become the next Executive Director of Opportunities for Broome – for him, the kiss of death. He had organized opposition to my continuation at the agency, hoping to secure the position for himself; now, thanks to my recommendation, that would never happen.

The reason for my concern about securing a new position was that the placement agency I was calling daily kept informing me that there were no suitable vacant positions in economics or business administration available immediately. Now that a new semester had begun, every institution had filled its vacancies. In a few cases, part time faculty had been hired, but those people were now under contract and could not be replaced at once. It appeared that, as far as an academic opening went, I was totally out of luck for now.

Two things happened then which restored my faith in karma, fate, or, indeed, the Almighty. My attorney in Atlantic City called me to tell me he had now received the final portion of the out-of-court settlement reached with Atlantic College over my non-reappointment there. I had previously received part of that settlement, but the College had had to pay it out over two years for budgetary reasons. The five-figure agreement was compensation for their violation of my civil and constitutional rights of free speech, as well as my academic freedom to advocate against legalized gambling. Those funds would relieve me of some time pressure to find a new position and sell my old home.

The second event was even more important to the direction which my life would take. An old friend, Norman, who had worked for many years for an Israeli agency, called me out of the blue, and asked, "Eugene, would you like to work professionally for the Israeli Finance Ministry? You would be based in Connecticut, in charge of the ministry's office which covers that State and Western Massachusetts. Your work would involve selling Israeli securities, staging programs, hosting Israeli visitors, and promoting Israel's image in your territory. You would have to be interviewed by the American national office of the Israeli Securities Agency in New York City, a branch of the Israeli Finance Ministry – but I have already sounded them out about this and they are enthusiastic about your background and capabilities. What do you say?"

What I said was that I was flabbergasted! The position in Connecticut was one way of accomplishing my commitment to my own people and their fledgling nation, to which I had considered emigrating some years earlier. But I also had the qualifications; I was an economist, had taken and taught numerous courses in finance at both the undergraduate and graduate levels, and had even had a summer job with a stockbroker in Dayton, Ohio.

The main credential which I lacked was the necessary certification from the National Association of Securities Dealers, who would require me to pass several tests and become a registered securities firm manager before I could be a full-fledged regional director for ISA, the Israeli Securities Agency, the American branch of Israel's Finance Ministry. However, I could accept the position provisionally, to be confirmed upon my passage of the necessary NASD examinations. And that is exactly what I decided to do, at once.

CHAPTER FIFTEEN

◆

MOVING AND TESTING

Luckily, I had accumulated some leave time at Opportunities for Broome, as I had tended not to take the full vacation time which I was allowed. Since my time there was now becoming unpleasant, in the light of my imminent and permanent departure, I was happy to take off the following Monday for an interview at the Israeli Securities Agency offices, then located in Lower Manhattan. They had offered to put me up at the Waldorf Astoria Hotel the night before the interview, and I had a lovely and leisurely dinner at the Waldorf, followed by a totally restful night in advance of my vital ISA interview.

I found that I still remembered the New York subway system from living there in my youth. Arriving promptly at the ISA offices for my interview, the first thing I discovered was their very tight security. I had to first sign in at a register in their building lobby before being escorted upstairs by an ISA security guard after checking my photo ID. I commended that guard on their very thorough screening of visitors, and he responded that they screened everybody, due to previous attempted "incidents" at their offices.

The next staff member I met was Nate, the ISA personnel director (the Human Resources designation was not yet in vogue). He was a retired Air Force officer who had had similar responsibilities in the military. He had already been contacted by my friend Norman, a long-term ISA staffer, and had been told that the Israeli Finance Ministry itself wanted me to be considered for their Connecticut directorship. Nate was a bit resentful of their interference, and therefore made clear that I would not be given any other "breaks" for the position. Rather, my employment would be only provisional until passing the tests which the National Association of Securities Dealers required for certification, with a score of at least eighty percent, since I would be a regional manager. Further, I would be on six months' probation, as was the case with all new regional directors. Nate then named a salary figure nearly twice what I had been earning at Opportunities for Broome, which softened the negative effect of his previous comments considerably. I then formally accepted the position of director of the Connecticut and Western Massachusetts office of the Israeli Securities Agency, completing a great deal of required paperwork. Nate congratulated me for taking on such a challenging post.

That next weekend, I traveled to Connecticut, a trip of some six or seven hours, and visited my new office at Bishop's Corner, a large shopping center in West Hartford. The staff had left an office key for me at the delicatessen in the back of the office building, and I was quite impressed with the office's carpeted floors and elegant furnishings – after the sparse OFB setup. This office was in a relatively-new building over a bank, rather than in the basement of an old church in Binghamton. The staff had left me a host of materials about the history and present activities of the Israeli Securities Agency, which I needed to study. They had also left me the preparatory materials which the previous director had used to take the required NASD certification tests. Even before taking over this new position at the start of the following month, I had my work cut out for me. This job was indeed going to be a real challenge, in more ways than I could possibly have realized.

I spent the remainder of that weekend looking for suitable housing, taking into account my West Hartford job location. I decided to rent an apartment for a year, during which I could take time finding a suitable house. There were few affordable rentals in West Hartford itself, but up the road a few miles in Bloomfield I located an apartment in a four-family building on Talcott View Road. The landlord met me there, showed me the available apartment, and I signed on the spot. It was good to be settling in so rapidly!

The Israeli Securities Agency had a policy of paying for all moving expenses, allowing the luxury of letting the movers do the packing in Tunnel, New York. I would really miss my old house there, built in 1828; but life moves on, and so did I. In early December, I was invited to the Binghamton Country Club for what I believed to be a "goodbye dinner" with Ted, a former chairman of the OFB Board and local attorney who had supported me throughout my fight to retain my job at the agency. Imagine the great surprise when Ted met us at the club and escorted us to a private room occupied by several dozen loyal OFB Board and staff members. I had not known there were so many people who had been in my corner, all feeling that I was getting a really raw deal for sticking to my principles. It was a great dinner, with some great speeches, as well as a most meaningful and deeply appreciated way to end my role in the War against Poverty.

The next morning, a Saturday, I was on the road to Bloomfield, Connecticut, in my old Imperial followed by a moving van. I supervised the unloading and placement of furniture in the new apartment, while most of the boxes were put in the basement. I had been studying the necessary NASD materials and sample tests intensely since the first trip to Connecticut, as I wanted to start working as a regional director of the Israeli Securities Agency with the required NASD tests completed. To have them hanging over me would detract and distract from my learning the job itself, so I had scheduled the tests for the Monday after our move. Nate, the ISA personnel director, had advised me against doing this, as I would have to wait thirty days to take the tests again if I failed them. Nate felt that I was moving too fast, based on past experience; and he told me so on the phone.

The tests were given at a training facility in Glastonbury, a suburb of Hartford, which had touch-screen format testing machines. There were one hundred multiple choice questions covering all areas of finance, economics, the securities industry, and its many rules and regulations. Upon completion of the test, the score was given at once on the screen. The test took two hours, and I needed all of that time to get through it and review my answers. The result was a score over the required eighty percent, sufficient to remove my status as only a provisional employee of the Israeli Securities Agency. I would be on six months' probation, as were all new regional managers – but at least I was fully on board.

CHAPTER SIXTEEN

◈

THE GENERAL

Working at the Israeli Securities Agency, or ISA, was a totally different experience from any other position I had held. My primary responsibility was to market a wide variety of Israeli securities. Some were not terribly attractive financially, and were mostly marketed to the Jewish community and to other supporters of Israel, including some fundamentalist Christian groups. Larger Bonds, starting at $25,000, floated with the prime rate, which was in the double digits during that period of the early 1980s. These newer bonds were quite serious investments and were heavily-marketed to financial and other institutions, as well as to some State governments. Since these securities were sold on their investment merits, which included early redemption provisions, they had become a major ISA focus.

However, we did not spend all of our time marketing securities; my office was the primary promoter of Israel's economic development activities in both Connecticut and Western Massachusetts, assisted by a satellite office in New Haven. We also conducted a host of programs to enhance Israel's image and to develop support and a positive view of Israel throughout my entire region. We were, indeed, a multi-faceted operation – but it did not take me long to learn that higher securities sales were "the bottom line" at ISA.

Achieving those higher securities sales goals was not difficult, as the office had been run in a lethargic fashion for some years prior to my arrival. The most recent director before me had actually been living in the office, having lost the lease on his apartment. His total sales of all our securities was under two million dollars a year when I arrived, and he had already left the scene. In my first few years with ISA there, sales increased exponentially, to first four million dollars, then to eight million dollars, and a year later to well over twelve million dollars annually. I had become the "fair-haired boy" of the Israeli Securities Agency, and my work had come to the attention of our national president, a retired Israeli General, who had been appointed by the Israeli Finance Ministry to a three-year term of office, renewable for a second term if things went well.

Having met The General, as everybody called him, at various staff meetings and conferences, usually in New York City or at one of the New York airports, I had found him to be a fascinating character. Born in Shanghai, China (I discovered he was just three days older than I), his family emigrated to Yemen due to the intense pressure being put on the Chinese Jewish community at that time. When even worse conditions for Jews began to prevail in Yemen, they then moved to Israel a few years later, and The General completed school and joined the Israeli Defense Forces. His career was highly successful, leading to a post in charge of all logistics and supply for the IDF and earning him the rank of General.

Upon his retirement from the military, General Yehudah was appointed head of the Israeli Securities Agency by the Finance Minister. I found him to be highly competent and dedicated, as well as a fascinating person, and we became good friends. Yehudah was always very considerate of his staff, tracking our life events and then contacting each of us to convey his personal regards. Early in my first year with ISA, at a staff meeting in New York, he asked me if it would be convenient for him to visit my office in West Hartford the following month, a visit which had been planned for some time and finally confirmed by a phone call. The General was a hands-on manager who visited all of our field offices periodically, and I told him that he would be most welcome and that I would arrange for him to meet our top leadership people throughout my region.

Upon hanging up the phone, however, I began to feel quite nervous about the amount of preparatory work which would be needed in advance of The General's visit. I decided that the most efficient approach would be to set up a reception at the Parkview Hilton Hotel in downtown Hartford, which was owned by David Chase, a top developer and Holocaust survivor; Roger Freedman, the husband of Chase's daughter Cheryl, chaired my Hartford ISA campaign and readily agreed to hosting the reception at the family hotel. I also arranged a press conference for all print and electronic news media just before the reception, featuring The General and helping to enhance Israel's image.

When The General arrived at Bradley International Airport, I picked him up and welcomed him on his first visit to the ISA Connecticut region. After visiting my office in West Hartford, where The General met our staff and reviewed our records, we arrived at the Parkview Hilton without incident, and I checked him in to the hotel. After making sure that all arrangements were in place for both the press conference and the ISA's area leadership reception, I went home for a bit of rest myself.

It was a glowing evening; the press conference went quite well, and The General was featured on the evening news on Channel 3, WTIC Television, which was conveniently also owned by David Chase and his family. The reception was attended by virtually all the leadership of ISA campaigns throughout Connecticut and Western Massachusetts. The food was wonderful and strictly kosher, as we had brought in a top caterer for the occasion. After I introduced The General to each guest upon arrival, he mingled with them and was careful to spend a bit of time with each of over-fifty attendees. I was impressed with his social skills, thinking that if his military prowess matched those skills, his rise to such an exalted rank in the Israeli Defense Forces was surely understandable. ISA was indeed lucky to have such a competent and personable leader, and I was lucky to work with him as a colleague who had become a friend.

CHAPTER SEVENTEEN

◆

MISSION

After driving The General to the airport the following morning, so that he could take his flight back to New York City and then return to the ISA headquarters, I decided that instead of returning to my office at once that day, I would try to get some rest at home first. Usually, I was in the office by 8 a.m., an hour before it opened, in preparation for the day's activities. This time, however, I called in from home and thanked the staff for their cooperation, telling them our office had made a good impression on The General.

The following day, I called The General in New York and told him how much the ISA leadership in my region had appreciated his outstanding visit. Surprisingly, his comment was that he also appreciated all the efforts of our area office, and he wished to show that appreciation in a very concrete way: he was inviting me to join the upcoming ISA Leadership Mission to Israel. I accepted instantly and enthusiastically, as I had been hoping for such an opportunity ever since learning of these periodic Missions to Israel when my friend Norman recruited me for ISA. While ISA staff normally made the trip once every five years at ISA expense, that delay could be waived in special instances. Apparently, such a waiver was being applied in my case, and I did not want to miss the opportunity.

The General replied that the details would be handled by our top travel official, nicknamed Mr. Israel, a legendary executive at the Israeli Securities Agency who was one of the first people hired when the ISA branch of the Israeli Finance Ministry was established in 1951. Mr. Israel had the unique credential of having arranged for former American First Lady Eleanor Roosevelt's trip to Israel while she was volunteering on behalf of our agency, to raise vital investment funds. He was already aware that I was to be scheduled to visit Israel on the very next Mission.

Mr. Israel faxed me a complete itinerary for a two-week "Mission" (as all of our trips were called) scheduled for June of 1983. I would be joining a group of ISA's top New York City leadership; since I was based in adjacent Connecticut, the full group would come from the same general area. Most of those on this mission were "heavy hitters" who invested in large amounts of ISA securities each year; but since I was going in my staff capacity, being a "heavy hitter" was not required of me, which was a good thing. While I did manage to make modest investments, the most I had done so far at ISA was to use part of my final legal settlement from Atlantic College for their securities.

When the time for the Mission arrived, I left Bradley International Airport north of Hartford to catch a connecting flight to JFK airport in New York, where our Mission assembled in the El Al Israel Airline lounge. We all arrived several hours before the flight, for briefings and photo opportunities. Mr. Israel himself, who had been to Israel more times than anyone else at ISA, was conducting the Mission.

After the El Al (meaning Up and Away) plane took off smoothly, I leaned back in my seat and opened my personal copy of the itinerary packet given to each participant, including some "special arrangements" which were not specified. Since I was a staff member, it was not unusual that special arrangements applied to my visit – but it turned out that those arrangements were so special and memorable that they would lead to a new phase of my life.

It was a long flight in those days, nearly eleven hours on the El Al Turboprop plane. Luckily, our group had been placed together in business class, so that there was sufficient legroom to avoid cramps, and a separate bathroom as well. My seatmate was Ruby, the director of the ISA West Palm Beach, Florida office. Ruby happened to be related to

Mr. Israel, our travel director, and was another early staff member for ISA who was now approaching retirement. He and I had struck up a friendship at staff meetings, as he was also one of the founders of our Professional Personnel Group, the staff organization for ISA mid-level executives, which functioned as a union to improve our situation. Ruby commented that he had not received the same manila envelope as I had, wondering if I were being singled out for "special treatment" of some sort. I did not rise to this bait.

As our plane began to descend over Israel, Ruby told me to look out of the window so as to see something very special. I then noted that the Israeli borders could be seen from the air; on the East and the North there were strips of green trees, while on the West was the Mediterranean, and on the South the Negev Desert. I had not known that Israel could be delineated from the air. Then, as I watched our descent, the Israeli national anthem, Hatikvah, The Hope, began to play in the cabin – and I suddenly found myself in tears. This was truly a Homecoming to a homeland I had never even known, and I was deeply moved.

CHAPTER EIGHTEEN

◆

ISRAEL

I discovered, early during my visit to Israel, that there is an Israeli adage which turned out to be true: "In Tel Aviv they play, in Jerusalem they pray, and in Haifa, they work." We had a tour bus at our disposal, and were driven from Ben Gurion Airport to the Tel Aviv Hilton, right on the Mediterranean. After a five-star dinner at the hotel, we walked along the lovely beach on that warm June night, watching Israelis socializing, playing volleyball, dancing to boom boxes, and sometimes just sitting quietly or reading. What struck me most of all was the wide diversity of the Israelis, which is far from what most Americans believe. While some were obviously of European extraction, fair-skinned and Western-looking, there were Orientals, Israeli Arabs, and even Black Israelis from North Africa. And while Hebrew was the predominant language (which I had studied somewhat in preparation for this trip), English was heard often, along with many other tongues. The Soviet Union had just begun to loosen its bizarre emigration restrictions, and occasionally I heard Russian speech and the strains of Russian Music. It was thus that I discovered that Israel was an amalgam of new Israelis from all over the world.

One thing which our group discovered, the next day, was that our tour bus left at six in the morning, and that there were no excuses for being late. My colleague from West Palm Beach, Ruby, had been designated as the "tour leader" – in which capacity he was the ramrod who routed us out of the hotel breakfast room or lobby and onto the bus, keeping count to be sure that nobody was left behind. Not surprisingly, Mr. Israel was first on the bus, along with our tour guide, an Israeli of Turkish descent named Ido, and our driver, Yankel, a holocaust survivor who had escaped Auschwitz and drove as if the Nazis were still chasing him.

From Tel Aviv we headed up into the Judean hills towards Jerusalem. As we neared that fabled city, we noted groves of thousands upon thousands of trees, ranging from pines to palms. These were all planted as part of the national forestation program. I also noted some bare patches on those hills, where the trees had been burned into ugly stumps. When I asked our guide, Ido, about this, he shook his head sadly, commenting, "Some of our opponents feel that Israeli trees are their enemies, as much as are Israeli humans. That is truly sad." Looking at those burned patches, I found myself becoming angry; trees had always been sacred to my family, indeed my mother chose her apartment in New York because of a large weeping willow tree in its courtyard, saying, "Now, I will always have a friend here." The idea of punishing innocent trees over real or imagined grievances was truly hurtful and hateful to me. Still, I strove to keep some perspective; the tree-burners must have had their reasons, and I wanted to learn what those reasons were.

Jerusalem is situated on seven hills, and has grown into a modern metropolis which now surrounds the fabled Old City. We went first to the Western Wall, the only remainder of the Second Temple of Biblical times, which had been part of Arab East Jerusalem until the Old City was liberated (as Israelis saw it) during the 1967 Six Day War with the Arabs. It was only then that I learned that we had arrived on the exact anniversary of that early June liberation, and that there was much extra chanting and rejoicing for that reason. Upon approaching and first touching the Western Wall, I found myself crying again. I left a prayer for peace in a crack in the Wall, an old Israeli custom.

For the next two days, we toured Jerusalem and its environs. The Knesset, or Israeli Parliament, was quite impressive with its glorious windows by artist Marc Chagall; we were able to sit in the visitors' gallery and try to follow a debate in Hebrew. We saw several archaeological digs, a special interest of Ido, our guide, who was a professor of archaeology at Hebrew University during the school year. Walking inside the walls of the Old City made me feel the weight of history on my own shoulders, as I pondered how many events, over thousands of years, had occurred nearby. Late dinner at the Jerusalem Hilton ended our first day there.

The next morning, we rode on the bus to Bethlehem, to see the Church of the Nativity and other Christian holy sites. Perhaps I should mention that our tour members, like the staff of the Development Corporation for Israel, were drawn from all religions and races. We had Christians and Moslems on the tour along with Jews, and Blacks, Hispanics, and even a couple of Orientals, along with the Caucasians. Having observed this diversity on my visits to the ISA national office in New York City, I was not surprised that it occurred also on this mission to Israel. We were a mini-United Nations and all got along very well.

Every day in Jerusalem, we ate in a special dining room of the Jerusalem Hilton Hotel, where a magnificent buffet called the Sabra Breakfast is served daily (a Sabra is a native of Israel, a term coined after the prickly pear cactus of the same name which grows there). We overate herring, whitefish, lox, boiled eggs, oatmeal, all sorts of breads, muffins and pastry, and lots of strong coffee. Our other meals were equally luscious.

The first stop on our itinerary was the Foreign Ministry itself, for a briefing by several top officials as to the present status of U.S.-Israeli relations. The briefing covered foreign aid, issues between the two allies, public opinion and media views, and similar topics. It took about two hours, and was conducted in English for our convenience. A very lively question-and-answer period concluded the briefing, providing much food for thought as we boarded our bus and continued our Mission.

CHAPTER NINETEEN

◈

MASADA

Following the briefing, we headed South from Jerusalem on a busy highway dominated by the Israelis' aggressive driving style. After about ten kilometers, we branched off onto a two-lane road lined with olive trees which led to a gated driveway with the words Neve Shalom, the new peace, on the gate. Tour guide Ido said, "Welcome to my family's kibbutz; we will have lunch here."

Luckily, I had brought some small gifts with me from the United States, having heard that it is the custom to present a token of appreciation when one is entertained in Israel. My briefcase contained some key chains and other memorabilia, which I took out before reaching Ido's modest home, where we were greeted by his wife and their youngsters. He also had older children, but they were in the kibbutz school. His wife was a Sabra, a native Israeli, whose English was a bit halting, but she certainly made us feel welcome. After a delicious dairy lunch (meat and dairy items are never mixed by observant Jews), Ido gave us a tour of his kibbutz, which specialized in growing vegetables and flowers, the latter being a cash crop which was exported to several European nations.

I was impressed that the kibbutz was essentially independent and self-reliant; nearly all needs could be met on-site, as food, housing, simple clothing, sandals, and even wine were produced there. An irrigation system provided sufficient water for the crops, and a spring provided water for the several hundred kibbutz residents. Children were raised collectively, one of the more controversial aspects of kibbutz life, but everyone seemed happy. Our group returned to the Jerusalem Hilton in time for dinner and discussion.

Early the following morning, we and our Mission headed Southeast towards the Dead Sea region of Israel. The terrain became increasingly bare and bleak, as we approached the Judean Desert. Then, a large and high rock formation loomed in the distance, which I recognized from pictures I had seen when I had studied Israel's history and geography. Noting my recognition, tour guide Ido told me, "Yes, that is Masada, the Fortress, a very special place for Israelis, and perhaps for you as well, Eugene."

We had brought a picnic lunch, which we carried up the winding trail leading to the flat top of Masada, some four hundred meters above the surrounding desert. There were quite a few visitors on that trail, and we exchanged greetings not only with Israelis, but with people from Europe and North America as well. Upon reaching the top, we drank from our water bottles, and then refilled them at the drinking fountains provided by the Masada government authority. Sitting in the sparse shade, Ido asked us what we knew of the site.

I replied that I was aware of how King Herod the Great, as he had termed himself, had feared a revolt against his rule on behalf of the Roman rulers of Israel – and so had fortified Masada between 37 and 31 BCE*. While that revolt never came in Herod's time, in 66 CE* the first Jewish-Roman War began, and a group of Jewish extremists called Sicarii or Zealots fled from Jerusalem with their families and overthrew the small Roman garrison at Masada. The Sicarii were more militant than most Zealots, and under the command of Elazar Ben Ya'ir, began attacking the area's Roman settlements. In 72 CE the Roman governor Lucius Flavius Silva marched with his troops and began building a road up Masada. (*BCE=Before Common Era or BC; CE=Common Era or AD.)

Completing the Roman Road took several years. There was continuous harassment from the Zealots on Masada, but the Romans were both patient and excellent engineers. As they neared the top of Masada, it was clear that the Zealots and their families would all be killed or taken into slavery: men, women, and children. Preferring to die as free people, they arranged a mass suicide, by the use of knives, resulting in 953 who died and only seven who were captured. This story, as recorded by the historian Josephus, was considered by the Israelis to be a victory of honor over oppression, and had always been venerated.

Mr. Israel, the ISA co-founder and top staffer on our Mission, then took me aside and sked me privately for my reaction to the tale of Masada. I paused for a moment, thinking about how to respond, and then said, "Well, chaver, since you asked, I think the Zealots over-reacted to the Roman threat. Had they not been raiding villages and picking off Roman troops when and where they could, Lucius Flavius Silva would not have taken several years, great resources, and effort to conquer Masada. The Zealots would probably have been left in peace – but, then again, not in true freedom. Perhaps they did what they had to do, but suicide pacts have never made much sense to me."

I wondered how Mr. Israel would react to this critique of what had become an Israeli legend – but instead of reacting directly, he asked me to follow him to the fortifications on top of Masada. Pointing to a small natural amphitheatre, he told me that when Israelis entered military service in the Israeli Air Force, they stood on that spot to take their oath, freely translated into English as: "May Masada never fall again." Then I realized that Masada was a symbol for Jewish perseverance and continuity, up to the present time. I therefore regretted my earlier comments, and asked what I might do to make up for them. Mr. Israel replied by reading the Special Oath to me in Hebrew, and I assented to it in that same language, adding under my breath: **"And may Israel never fall again, either."**

After the long walk back down Masada, we drove to an elegant Dead Sea hotel for dinner and a late swim in those buoyant waters, which are supposed to have healing properties. Mr. Israel had arranged for rooms for us at the hotel that night, courtesy of the Israeli Foreign Ministry, as he told us that we would go to Eilat, on the Red Sea at the Southern tip of Israel, the following day. We were to visit a small naval facility there.

As matters turned out the next day, we received a briefing from a young Israeli naval officer who commanded a small patrol boat at Eilat. His patrol boat was a leftover from the Vietnam War, which had been turned over to Israel by the U.S. government. That briefing, however, was interrupted as a siren went off and we had to leave the ship at once as it was going out into the Red Sea, due to reports of possible infiltrators from Egypt who had entered Israeli waters. The next day, Israeli newspapers carried stories about how our young captain and his crew had intercepted a shipment of illegal drugs and arrested the drug runners. Other times, they intercepted terrorists heading to attack Israel.

We returned to Jerusalem and, over the next few days, visited the Golan Heights, on the Israeli border with Syria and the only location where winter snow was not unusual. We spent some time in the tunnels used for protection from Syrian shells lobbed into the North of Israel, met with the commander of the Golan Heights forces, and saw several towns which also came under frequent attack from the North.

We also visited the Lebanese border, then separated from Israel by what was termed The Good Fence. Lebanese citizens could come through that fence to see relatives on the Israeli side of the border, to get better medical care in Israel than what was available in Lebanon, or to engage in trade and business. I told Tour guide Ido that I only wished the Syrian border became peaceful, similar to that with Lebanon, to which he responded, "Unfortunately, there is no Good Fence with Syria. Lebanon is likely to be the next Arab nation to make peace with Israel; at least, we hope so. Syria is much more likely to be the last."

It had become more and more obvious to me that Israel was at severe risk of attack, having already suffered from five wars and endless sniping in between, as surrounding Arab nations tried to totally destroy the Jewish State. Each time, though, Israel had been able to survive, and (as in the 1967 Six Day War) even win back additional territory. It was even believed by many Israelis, and the nation's supporters elsewhere, that this was the result of Divine Intervention, about which I have always had an open mind. Now, near the end of my time in Israel, I had learned the truth about how this fledgling nation had developed and acquired nuclear bombs: a capacity which discouraged future wars.

Our group was visiting the Israeli atomic power plant at Dimona, a closely-guarded facility, and our guide was one "Shimshon," the Hebrew version of Simon and perhaps not his original name at all, as he had come to Israel from the Soviet Union some years earlier. Since my own American Jewish communities had been in the business of taking former Soviet Jews for re-settlement, while many others went to Israel starting in the 1980s, I asked Shimshon over lunch how he had managed to get out of the Soviet Union. He replied, "Actually, the Soviets made a mistake letting me go; I was confused with someone else who also had my same Russian name. Had that not occurred, I would never have been allowed to leave, as I had been a Soviet nuclear scientist. When I managed to reach Israel, I helped our nuclear experts here develop atomic weapons, using much that I had learned in the Soviet Union to do so. It truly was justice; had our people been treated decently in the Soviet Union, few would have chosen to leave. But that was not the case; we were often detested and despised, just as we had been under the Czars long before. I am proud that I helped my own people develop The Bomb here in Israel; we really need it to defend ourselves. **Am Yisrael Chai – the people of Israel live!**"

CHAPTER TWENTY

◆

"NUSUB" PROPOSAL

In two more days, the Israeli Securities Agency Mission would travel on to Haifa, where we would be studying Israeli industry and commerce. On our next-to-last day in Jerusalem, we visited a scale model of the Second Temple, which in reality once stood in Jerusalem until destroyed by the Romans in 70 C.E. The Western Wall of that Temple was all that remained now – but judging from the model, it had once been magnificent! We went to several outstanding museums in Jerusalem, ending at Yad Vashem, Israel's Holocaust memorial and museum. I was able to pay my respects to Raul Wallenberg, the Swedish diplomat who had saved thousands of Jews during World War II by having Swedish passports issued to them so that they could escape the Nazis. Wallenberg had disappeared into Soviet territory as the war ended, probably being abducted, and never returned. His lifesaving efforts were noted by a tree planted in his name in a special grove at Yad Vashem dedicated to non-Jews who saved people during the Holocaust. Unfortunately, there are not very many trees in that grove, reminding me of my own oath.

As our final day in Jerusalem dawned, without any explanation of that day's activities, I thought it likely that there was something special planned for each of us on the Mission; in that expectation, I was not to be disappointed. When I asked about our plans for that final day, Tour guide Ido told me that he would be escorting me to the headquarters of the IDF, the Israeli Defense Forces, where I was to meet with some top military officials. When I tried to pump him as to what they could possibly want from me, he said, "All in good time." I replied that the "good time" had better be "at once", as I was very puzzled.

Security was very tight at the IDF headquarters; I was searched and my fingerprints were compared with a set which I had had to provide in the United States as manager of our securities firm's Connecticut office. Since those U.S. fingerprints had been faxed in advance to the IDF, I noted how close the cooperation was between the two allies. Once my identity was confirmed, a young soldier (nearly all of them seemed so young) led us to a small conference room and left us alone there. A few minutes later, an Israeli officer entered and introduced himself merely as Dan. He was wearing fatigues and had sandy hair and a stocky build, but bore an air of command about him. I waited expectantly.

Dan then asked Ido if I had been briefed about the purpose of the meeting, and Ido replied that he understood that Dan would do the briefing. Looking into my eyes, Dan then said, "We would like you to help Israel obtain a nuclear submarine for our navy." I first gasped and then, unfortunately, laughed, saying, "You surely cannot be serious." I had not intended to be rude, but Dan's statement appeared totally ridiculous. I thought that I must have heard him incorrectly, particularly as he had a heavy accent.

Ido, who had a military background himself (as did many Israelis) spoke up at this awkward moment, saying, "Eugene, please hear Dan out. Your Mission has spent the past week together so that you could see and understand our difficult situation as fully as possible. We had planned on introducing this subject at the Eilat naval base; but as you know, events intervened there and we had to change our plans. Nevertheless, we are indeed making a serious proposal to you, since you can play a unique role in this matter."

Dan then continued, "We understand that you know a Connecticut developer, Jacob Jacobson, through your professional work for the Israeli Securities Agency. Could you tell me about your relationship with Mr. Jacobson?"

I responded that Jacob was a major developer of office buildings, hotels, shopping centers, and other properties throughout the Eastern United States, as well as a major philanthropist and supporter of ISA. He was a member of our leadership cabinet, and I had worked closely with him in approaching other developers as well as Holocaust survivors, because Jacob was himself a Polish survivor of the Nazis.

Dan then asked me if I were aware that Jacob owned all of the land adjacent to the North of the U.S. Naval Submarine Base in Groton, Connecticut, where he was planning on building a major shopping center for that growing area. I told him that I had not been aware of that aspect of Jacob's business interests, and wondered what it had to do with me – or with Israel. Dan replied that the Israeli Navy needed a nuclear submarine, as their few diesel submarines were quite obsolete and incapable of "doing what needed to be done." Jacob could be the key to getting the U.S. Navy to turn over an older nuclear submarine to Israel – and I could be the key to getting Jacob to make that request. The American Navy badly wanted Jacob's land adjacent to the present Submarine Base, since there was no other way that they could expand the base. What I was being asked to do, therefore, was to approach Jacob and to get him to offer that piece of land to the Navy, gratis, in exchange for a commitment to a nuclear sub for Israel.

While I found this proposal amazing, the idea was not totally foreign to me, as my father had been in the aircraft component section of the American defense industry, and I had worked at his company for several summers as a youth. I recalled conversations about ways we could deal with the U.S. Air Force, some of them nearly as bizarre as Dan's proposal to help Israel to obtain a nuclear submarine. But I also recalled that most of those schemes never went through, and that my father had come to regret a few which had appeared to work but had later backfired. I shared these views with Dan and Ido. Dan asked me if I were saying "No" to the nuclear submarine proposal by my comments.

I then stated that I was not rejecting the nuclear sub project out of hand, but rather was raising some objections which would have to be answered before I could approach Jacob. Nevertheless, if the proposal were refined and made more appealing to the various parties involved, particularly Jacob and the top submarine command in the U.S. Navy, it just might work. Dan then asked if I would be willing to give it a try, in terms of at least broaching the matter to Jacob and, if he would consider it, then arranging a meeting at the Israeli Consulate in New York with their military attaches. I gave a conditional positive response, and we worked for the remainder of that day on pinning down the details of my approach to Jacob.

That afternoon, following the extended meeting at the Israeli Defense Ministry, Dan used a military car to drive Ido and myself North along the Mediterranean coast to Haifa, where I checked into the Crowne Plaza Hotel, rejoining the ISA mission that evening. The group tried to pump me about what I had been doing while they were touring Northern Israel, and I first tried evasion. When that did not work, I said, jocularly, that I had been recruited into the Israeli secret service – knowing that they would never believe such a wild story in a million years. I was right about their disbelief, as my friend Ruby, the mission leader, remarked that I had probably been "shacked up with a Sabra", an Israeli native, while they were on a hot bus or out in the hot sun. I was quite content to let my friends believe whatever they wished, as long as they did not suspect the truth.

After two days in Haifa, studying Israel's great commercial and industrial progress, and visiting the Weizmann Institute of Science, which reminded me of my days at MIT, we returned to Ben Gurion Airport and reluctantly boarded our El Al return flight to New York. I was somewhat pensive on the return trip, thinking about the special assignment I had agreed to undertake, and about what I would say to Jacob as to trying to get Israel a nuclear submarine. As we approached the American coastline, and then New York City, that entire matter seemed more and more dubious, yet I could not forget or dismiss it.

CHAPTER TWENTY-ONE

◆

JACOB

I had returned from Israel on the last Sunday in June. Recuperating from the hectic mission and the long flights home would have justified my coming to work late next Monday, but I knew that I would need to start working on what I now called the "nusub plan" – an acronym for nuclear submarine, but not so obvious as to be risky.

I made an appointment to see Jacob Jacobson the following day. Jacob had an elegant suite taking up the entire eighteenth floor of an office tower in Hartford, which his company had built. He chose that particular floor because the number eighteen was Chai in Hebrew, meaning life. Jacob was a devout believer in the power of life, having survived the Nazi's Auschwitz concentration camp; then he escaped while being transported to another camp, joined the partisans and fought against the Nazis in Poland for the rest of World War II. Emigrating to the United States as a refugee after the War, he had begun his new life by laying flooring tiles in Hartford, while saving his money, buying that business, and ultimately becoming a major developer throughout New England. He was now a multi-millionaire who could relate to people from all nations and backgrounds.

When I was ushered into his inner sanctum, Jacob first asked me about my mission to Israel, and we talked about developments there for a few minutes. Then he said, "Eugene, my secretary told me that you said you needed to see me urgently, so I believe your request must be related to something which happened in Israel. What is it you wish of me?"

I then outlined the proposal from the Israeli Defense Ministry, specifically their Navy, as to a trade of Jacob's substantial land holding adjacent to the U.S. Naval Submarine Base in Groton, Connecticut, for a nuclear submarine which was being decommissioned, to be provided to Israel. Jacob replied, "Having lived through so much in my life, I rarely hear something which surprises me, but you have my congratulations, as your proposal on behalf of the Israelis has astounded me."

Hearing that comment from Jacob, which he made with a very grave expression, I assumed that he was rejecting the very concept; therefore, I thanked him for his time and got up to leave. At that point, a smile broke out on his face, and he said, "Wait, Eugene. I am not rejecting the proposal just because it is astounding – it is fascinating as well. My dear friend Lou Rogow helped to establish the Israeli Air Force, in the early days, while running his aircraft company here. Perhaps I can perform a comparable task for the Israeli navy. I'm going to call my friend Hy Rickover, who is just retiring as a four-star admiral in the U.S. Navy. He and I were both born in Poland, and he is known as the Father of the Nuclear Navy in the United States. Hy Rickover will know what, if anything, I can do about this."

I had not expected to hear back from Jacob immediately. However, I was surprised to receive a call that Wednesday, two days later, from Jacob's secretary, asking me to see Jacob again, for lunch at his office that day. Jacob rarely took time off for an outside lunch, and it was an honor to be invited to join him then. It was even more of an honor when I discovered that his daughter and son-in-law, both of whom worked in the family development business, were also at our luncheon.

Jacob began by saying, "I've spoken to Hy Rickover, and he in turn sounded out the present leadership of the U.S. Navy, including the deputy secretary and senior officers. I had not been aware of how badly the Navy wants the land I own adjacent to the Sub Base in Groton – that is their only direction for expansion, as Long Island Sound blocks the West and South, and on the East there is a major Naval housing development. They are willing to explore the situation, but Hy says it would be a terribly long shot to get Israel a nuclear submarine, as normally anything like that would have to go through Congress. Still, Israel is our major Mideast ally, and it might not be impossible. A meeting will be set up at the Submarine Base, and you must attend, as you received the Israeli proposal firsthand."

This was far more positive than what I had expected, and I thanked Jacob and then asked him if I should arrange for an Israeli naval attaché to also attend. He replied that this would not be appropriate, and indeed it was vital that it appear that the project had originated at the American end rather than coming from Israeli officials. Nor did he wish to go to any meetings with consular officials in New York City. Rather, we were to leave it up to the U.S. Navy to set a date and time for that vital meeting at the Submarine Base.

The following week, I heard from Jacob Jacobson that the Navy wanted to meet during the last week of July, at the Submarine Base in Groton, and that everything was strictly confidential, indeed secret. The meeting was to be "off the record." Jacob knew that I would have to get more specifics of the Israeli proposal from their Naval attaché, but nobody else was to be told of the meeting.

The details of the "nusub" plan were ironed out the following week in New York. The Israeli Naval attaché said that he understood several older nuclear submarines were going to be decommissioned, taken out of service, over the next two years. The very first nuclear submarine, the Nautilus, had been made into a museum at the Submarine Base. If one of the others could be made available to Israel, and a crew trained at the U.S. Sub Base, they could in turn transport it to the Israeli naval base at Eilat. They would not need data on any secret nuclear technology, simply the "operational instructions", but would want an American nuclear engineer to accompany the Israeli crew on the voyage to Israel. The engineer would then be hired for up to two years to train Israelis in operating the reactor. Israeli Naval officers would learn how the operate the Submarine on the initial voyage to Eilat in Israel, later receiving further training and instruction as needed.

Many other specifics of the "nusub" proposal were discussed, and I was required to memorize all of them, as nothing could be put in writing at that point. Since no Israelis were invited to the meeting with U.S Navy officials, I had to carry the ball. Even after returning to Connecticut following the meeting, I continued to study up on the American nuclear navy, its submarines, and as much technical data as was publicly available. I began to be glad that I had spent two years studying engineering at MIT; that background came in handy. At that point, I did not share any "nusub" information with my employer, ISA, as I was sworn to silence about the project; it is truly said that "loose lips sink ships" – and submarine projects, too.

CHAPTER TWENTY ONE

◆

MEETING

On the day of the meeting, I drove to Jacob Jacobson's mansion in West Hartford; he was already awaiting me, with two cups of coffee, and we got into his Jaguar for the drive to the U.S. Naval Submarine Base in Groton. Most of the traffic was coming into Hartford at that hour of the morning, so we managed to make it through "Malfunction Junction" where Interstates 84 and 91 merged. As we headed down Route 2 towards the shore, Jacob asked me about my meeting with Israeli representatives in New York. I had been permitted to answer any questions he asked; since he was our "point man" for the "nusub" deal, he was an exception to the secrecy policy, and I provided the full details.

Jacob replied that I seemed to have covered all of the bases and that he wanted me to make the proposal to the Navy, as I was the person most familiar with what the Israelis wanted. I told him that this was a big responsibility, but that I would do my best. After a period of silence while we sipped our coffee, Jacob mused, "Little did I think, when I was in the Auschwitz Nazi concentration camp, that I would even survive, let alone be involved in such a project as this one. There was no State of Israel then, and probably there would not be an Israel now were it not for the Holocaust. It was the world's guilt, transmitted through the United Nations, which led to the narrow U.N. vote to create modern Israel."

Not knowing what to say in response to Jacob's musings, I was silent for a bit; then I asked him, "Do you think the creation of Israel was an act of divine providence, and that it took the murder of six million Jews to lead to that act? Surely that would be far too high a price to pay, in order for Jews to have a homeland." I told him that while in Israel I had visited the Yad Vashem Holocaust Memorial in Jerusalem and had been deeply moved. I had also seen the small grove of trees dedicated to non-Jews who saved Jewish lives; there were not very many trees in that grove; I wondered why so few had helped us.

Jacob then said, "Nobody who is not a firsthand survivor of the Nazis can understand what those of us who are survivors went through – and are still going through. Every day I ask myself why I am here, when my family and so many others are not. I have yet to find an answer to that question, and I doubt that I ever will. But, today, we have business to do with the U.S. Navy. Those unanswered questions will have to remain unanswered."

Upon reaching the Submarine Base and identifying ourselves to the Marine guards, who had been told to expect us, we were directed at once to the administration building and then escorted to a small conference room. A few minutes later, a door at the other end of the room opened and several naval officers entered – I recognized the Commander of the Sub Base from seeing his picture in news stories, then several aides – and then an elderly man walking with the help of a cane, a small white-haired man with erect posture. Though dressed in civilian clothing, he was unmistakable: Retired Admiral Hyman George Rickover, the "Father of the Nuclear Navy," was attending this historic meeting.

The Base Commander introduced himself and his aides, then saying, "The man on my right needs no introduction, because until his retirement recently, Admiral Rickover had given sixty-three years of continuous and distinguished service to the Navy. He was the longest-serving active-duty military officer in U.S. history, and is still a senior advisor."

With that introduction, Rickover smiled and said, "I don't know about the advisor part, but I am now definitely a senior!" The meeting convened without further ado.

Jacob Jacobson was asked to explain our proposal on behalf of the State of Israel, and I was extremely nervous as he turned to me, saying,

"Eugene will provide the specifics." Luckily, after years of teaching followed by the heavy public speaking required in more recent jobs, I was reasonably comfortable making such a presentation. Still, I had never before made such a case as I had to make now. I began by summarizing the history of American-Israeli friendship and the close alliance of the two nations, pointing out many instances where the nations had helped each other under various mutual assistance pacts.

Then, knowing that beating around the bush was not going to be helpful, I presented the specifics of what Israel wanted and needed: a nuclear submarine which was being taken out of service, the necessary stock of repair parts, full training, and also a nuclear engineer.

Jacob Jacobson then very tactfully explained that he really wanted to donate his land North of the Submarine Base, the only open land available for its vital expansion, to the U.S. Navy, quietly and with no fanfare. We had discussed in the car, driving down, that no impression of a "quid pro quo" be given, that there must never be any overt horse trading of a nuclear submarine for land rights; that would definitely queer the deal. All those on the Navy side at the meeting knew the facts, but some facts are better left unstated. Rather, and rather cleverly, Jacob said that there were certain requirements as to the land the Navy needed, which had to be cleared up before title could be passed to the Submarine Base Command, which might take a few months; that would allow time for our proposal to be further considered and a determination of its viability to take place.

Up to that point, everyone who spoke had been very polite and tactful – but Admiral Rickover had not yet spoken. Indeed, I had assumed he was to be an observer, probably invited as a tribute both to his long service and his friendship with Israel. Indeed, he had been the highest-ranking person of Jewish faith ever in the Navy.

But, when the other presentations were finished, Hy Rickover then stood up and spoke up, saying, "Gentlemen, let's cut the crap! The Navy needs this land, Israel needs a nuclear sub. It's as simple as that. We just have to find a way to make both things happen." With that, he sat down, and it was agreed that the Submarine Base commander would explore the matter with the Deputy Secretary of the Navy in Washington. We planned to meet again early in the fall for a progress report on those explorations. Meanwhile, Jacob Jacobson would work on clearing up any issues over the use of his land abutting the Submarine Base, such as zoning matters and the former proposal that it become a shopping center. The meeting closed on a high note.

Driving back to Hartford, Jacob told me that he thought the meeting had gone better than he had expected, saying, "Frankly, Eugene, I thought they would politely throw us off the Sub Base. Even after I spoke with Hy Rickover on the phone, I never dreamed they would consider the proposal seriously. Were it not for our retired admiral, they probably would not even have granted the meeting, let alone this real consideration. Now we will just have to wait and see. Please report what happened to your Israeli friends in New York, and tell them I did my best. Perhaps that will turn out to be one reason why I survived the Nazis, when so many others, indeed my whole family, were not so lucky."

CHAPTER TWENTY-THREE

◈

IMMINENT THREAT

Realizing that the wheels of government grind slowly, even when they do grind at all, Jacob and I knew it would probably be some time before the Navy made a decision on our request for a nuclear submarine to be provided to Israel. What we did not know, however, was the manner in which a totally-unexpected event would affect that request.

My own involvement in that event began in August with a visit to Connecticut for the Israeli Securities Agency by Chaim Yaron, an Israeli General who was on an American speaking tour. General Yaron was scheduled to make presentations in both Hartford and Springfield, Massachusetts. He was a tall but rather rotund man with an engaging smile and perfect English, who had had a distinguished career in the Israeli Air Force. During his visit to our area, he wished to meet with executives at several U.S. aircraft companies, such as Pratt and Whitney, which was based in Hartford as part of United Technologies conglomerate. I had a very busy three-day schedule planned for General Yaron.

After meeting General Yaron at Bradley Airport, we had a rather late dinner at the Airport Sheraton Hotel so that I could brief him on the various events scheduled for his visit. I had found that, particularly with the Israeli military, a thorough briefing was expected, and, indeed, required. In one instance when I had not prepared fully to present each and every tiniest detail of his arrangements to a retired ambassador who was visiting us, he had filed a complaint with my boss. I was determined that no such error would occur again.

General Yaron, though, was quite cordial, telling me to call him Chaim, which means "life" in Hebrew. We had had several drinks before dinner, as service in the hotel restaurant was slow at that time of night. Chaim then asked me about my trip to Israel in June, as I had met him briefly at the Good Fence between Lebanon and Israel on that trip. He was aware of some of the special arrangements made on the mission, and we talked at length about Israel's situation in the world, and particularly about Israeli-American relations – always a fascinating, if delicate, topic.

Chaim was probably influenced by the combination of cocktails and good red wine, as he relaxed after dinner and then told me, "Well, Eugene, matters behind the Good Fence on the Lebanese border are not so good now. Your American Marine component of the Multinational Peacekeeping Force in Lebanon is at severe risk of a bombing attack on their barracks. The command of those Marines has put all of its eggs in one basket there, as you Americans say. We have repeatedly warned your top Pentagon officials, even the Secretary of Defense, of the risks; but they merely shrug and say we are being silly, that nobody would dare to attack a United States Marine barracks. In that, they are totally wrong; it is only a matter of time until a terror attack occurs there, and that time is getting shorter with each passing day."

I must have shown shock on my face at General Yaron's calm statement; Israelis had lived with terrorism since the founding of that nation in 1948, and they took it in stride. But, in those days, we Americans were not nearly as familiar with such atrocities. I did know that Israel had invaded Lebanon in 1982 to put a stop to attacks on Northern Israel from there, organized by a terrorist group which now called itself Islamic Jihad but was probably part of the Hezbollah structure. After that initial military action, the United Nations had authorized a multi-national peacekeeping force made up of military personnel from the United States, France, and other nations. The American Marine contingent had a barracks near the Beirut airport. Apparently, that barracks was at risk.

Chaim then apologized for upsetting me, but I shrugged off the apology, telling him that he was not at fault; what had upset me was Israel's inability to get severe risks to several hundred Marines across to those in the Pentagon who could take immediate and strong protective action. I remembered learning of an incident involving an Israeli tank approaching the "green line" separating Beirut into several sections, when an American Army officer stepped out from a bunker and started waving a pistol around at the Israeli tank commander, telling him to back off. This incident had not been widely reported in the American press, as it made the American officer look like an utter idiot, but it had come to the attention of the Israeli Consulate in New York. Indeed, at the Consulate it was treated with some amusement – but the prospect of our forces being unprepared for a serious bomb attack was far from amusing; it was frightening. America needed that alert!

I debated what to do with Gen. Yaron's information throughout the three days of his visit to my territory, a visit which was quite successful. Indeed, his meeting with Pratt and Whitney Aircraft executives led to a tentative Israeli deal to purchase the Blackhawk helicopter, which he had seen in prototype during his visit.

After Chaim Yaron returned to New York, on his way back to Israel, I drove to the Hartford office of our Congresswoman, Barbara Kennelly, and learned that her Chief of Staff happened to be there before returning to Washington. We had recently staged a Tribute Dinner for Barbara Kennelly, and I had established an excellent relationship with her and all of her key staff.

Barbara Kennelly had just joined the United States Congress upon a special election to fill the vacancy created by the death of her predecessor, William R. Cotter. Our dinner in her honor celebrated her service as Connecticut's Secretary of the State from 1972 to 1982, as well as her joining the House of Representatives on January 12, 1982. I hoped that if anyone could get the American Government, particularly the Defense Department, to take the threats against our Marines in Lebanon seriously, it might be Rep. Kennelly.

I apologized to her Chief of Staff for barging in without an advance appointment, but asked if I could discuss a highly-confidential matter which was urgent. He escorted me to an inner office, closed the door, and then asked what could possibly be so urgent. I replied that the safety of our Marines in Beirut, Lebanon might well be compromised. Then, I gave him the details of what General Yaron had shared with me. He thought for a moment, and then told me that I really needed to speak directly with the Congresswoman, who was returning to her Hartford home that weekend; he would schedule me to see her.

CHAPTER TWENTY-FOUR

◆

REP. BARBARA KENNELLY

That Saturday, I drove to the Kennelly home near Hartford's Elizabeth Park. The late summer roses were still in bloom, and I could smell their sweetness as I passed the small pond and park gates nearby. The Kennelly home had been a landmark for decades. The Congresswoman was married to attorney James J. Kennelly, who was a State legislator. She was the daughter of John M. Bailey, the legendary head of Connecticut Democrats. She began her political career on the Hartford City Council in 1979, before running successfully for Secretary of the State, and then for the U.S. House of Representatives.

Barbara herself met me at the door, welcoming me to her family's residence. She thanked me again for the tribute dinner in her honor which the Israeli Securities Agency had staged at the Parkview Hilton Hotel, and for awarding her the Israel President's Medal for her public service and dedication both to Connecticut and to American-Israeli friendship. I replied that the honor was ours, and that I appreciated her seeing me on short notice, because the reason for my visit was a most urgent one.

Upon entering her living room, I found her husband and Congressional Chief of Staff also present. Without further ado, I explained what General Chaim Yaron had told me about the risks to our Marine contingent, in Beirut, Lebanon, on a peacekeeping mission. The Congresswoman and the others then asked a number of questions dealing with the exact nature of that risk, and what steps could be taken to reduce or eliminate it. Finding that I was perhaps out of my depth as to those specific steps, I recalled what I had seen in Israel as to the anti-terrorism precautions taken there.

Terrorism is a near-daily event in Israel, and such precautions have become second nature there. Virtually every Israeli serves in the Home Guard after mandatory military service. While some of the ultra-orthodox are allowed to perform national non-military service due to conscientious objection to war and other fighting, they may still participate in the Home Guard. While all of this might have been interesting, I could see that my audience was becoming impatient, as it did not seem to relate well to the Marines' risks.

Therefore, I made my comments more pointed, stating frankly that (in those times) America and Americans were totally naïve about terror tactics. We seemed to believe that "it can't happen here." In particular, from what General Yaron had told me, the information on the severe risks our Marines were facing had been presented to the Pentagon through Israeli military channels; those were threats which Israeli intelligence had uncovered. According to Chaim, the Pentagon had shrugged off that vital threat information, telling the Israelis essentially, "Don't worry about it; we aren't." Nothing had been done to secure the Marine Barracks, no other changes were made, watchfulness was not heightened; it was highly likely that the terrorists were well aware of those facts.

Barbara Kennelly is an imposing woman, tall, straight, with a tinge of silver in her hair. She listened attentively, as did her husband and Chief of Staff. Then she said, "Eugene, when I return to Washington on my Monday flight, the very first thing I will do is to ask for a private audience with the Secretary of Defense himself. It is likely that the Israeli information never reached him, or anyone else in top authority. Our military does not like to admit vulnerability; but, in this case, we must face the facts and the risks – otherwise, we will surely face the music!"

CHAPTER TWENTY-FIVE

◆

CAP WEINBERGER

The reigning Secretary of Defense, appointed by President Ronald Reagan upon Reagan's inauguration in January, 1981, was Caspar Willard Weinberger, known as "Cap" Weinberger to everyone, including the news media. Cap had been a close friend and confidant of the new president for decades, and had already amassed substantial public service credentials both in his home state of California and as part of the Nixon Administration, where he served as Director of the Office of Management and Budget, before becoming Secretary of Health, Education, and Welfare.

Weinberger's nickname had become "Cap the Knife" for his cost-cutting abilities in government service. Upon Nixon's ouster as President, he returned to the private sector as an official of the Bechtel Corporation and then as chairman of Hartford-based United Technologies. In that latter capacity, I had met Cap a couple of times at various regional meetings, and had not particularly liked either him or his approach to government. He was held in some contempt, as well, by the Jewish community, as Cap had Jewish roots via his father. It was said that, on the plane to Hartford to take over United Technologies, he had "lost his circumcision" and become an Episcopalian; actually, that conversion had happened much earlier.

Congresswoman Barbara Kennelly and her Chief of Staff secured a meeting with Cap the Knife early the following week, right after Labor

Day of 1983. How I would have loved to be a fly on the wall of that Pentagon office! As it was, I was in my own office in West Hartford, awaiting word of Weinberger's reaction to being told that U.S. Marines serving with the U.N. Peacekeeping Force in Lebanon were at risk of a terrorist attack.

Just before noon, the phone rang and my assistant told me that the Congresswoman herself was calling. I was surprised, expecting to hear from her Chief of Staff, which would be more in line with protocol. When I answered, Barbara Kennelly sounded defeated and sad. I asked her if the Secretary of Defense had doubted the validity of the Israeli warning. She replied, "Well, what surprised us was that Cap already knew of the threats against our Marines in Lebanon. It turns out that the Israeli Defense Minister had warned him personally, so we were not telling him anything he did not know. He told us that he had also already decided that the warning was exaggerated at best, and false at worst. He appears simply incapable of believing that any rag-tag terrorist group would challenge the might of American armed forces. I believe he is totally wrong, but cannot convince him; Cap Weinberger is as stubborn as they come, and in this case American troops may die as a result of that pigheaded stubbornness."

While telling her how deeply disappointed I was at Cap's reaction, I praised her efforts to prevent such an impending disaster of grave dimensions. I also told her I would confer with some Israeli contacts as to what further steps could be taken in this matter. The next day, I set up an appointment to discuss my regular securities sales campaign with the chiefs at our New York headquarters, as a cover for an emergency meeting with defense staff at the Israeli Consulate there.

Since the information on the risks to our Marines in Lebanon had come to me from an Israeli General who had perhaps had too much to drink, I was not sure how the Consulate staff would take my meddling in Israeli-American relations and security issues. It did not take long for me to find that out, as their defense attaché turned to me in astonishment and said, "Eugene, just who in Hell do you think you are? You have no authority to be negotiating Israel's foreign policy and Americans' security in this manner!"

Probably I was not at my best, as I responded, "Well, it may be a nasty job, but somebody had to do it. You Israelis are now sitting on this information, when you knew that Cap Weinberger is not a friend to Israel, that he is stubborn and pigheaded, and that he would ignore your official warnings. There is more you could and should have done!"

I suspected that the defense attaché did not have much enthusiasm for the small cadre of volunteers around North America who kept tabs on media coverage of the Middle East in general, and Israel in particular.

I also told him that I would not give up trying to protect the safety of our Marines in Beirut. I further stated that I was prepared to go to the New York Times headquarters, only a few blocks away from us, and repeat to them the story of the Israeli warning I had received: namely that our Marines were at severe risk of a bombing at their headquarters in Beirut, Lebanon – and that the U.S. Defense Department was doing nothing about it.

The Israeli then looked at me with ice in his eyes and said, "Were you to try that, the story would never be printed, as we have very good ties with the New York Times. And even the attempt would not be good for your health, Eugene." Those words were clearly a threat, and I must admit to becoming quite nervous. I had indeed faced threats before, in Atlantic City when I challenged the pro-gambling interests of the crime syndicate. In that case, I had survived – but those threats had been made by the "other side", the bad guys. I had not expected to be threatened by an Israeli official, as they were supposed to be the good guys.

After a moment's reflection, I said, "This meeting and this conversation are over. How dare you threaten me! When I was on my mission to Israel, I found that I loved that brave nation and its warmhearted people – but I could not love the vaunted Israeli arrogance. I realize that your arrogance comes in part as the result of the world's mistreatment, as Israelis see it, but you people need to be able to separate out your friends from your enemies. I have always been a friend, and will continue to be one. But I will not put up with attempted intimidation, nor will I be muzzled by you." I then rose and walked away, hoping that he would not follow me; going straight to Grand Central Station, I took the Conrail train back to Connecticut. My trip had been totally wasted.

CHAPTER TWENTY-SIX

◈

BEIRUT BOMBING

For the next few weeks, I nursed my hurt feelings while doing no further volunteer work for the State of Israel. I needed to re-think my relationship with the Israelis, and even with my employer, ISA itself. For many years, I had volunteered with various community agencies promoting Israeli-American relations. Now, I began to wonder if those efforts to bring two nations closer together were worthwhile, or had been in vain.

The entire situation changed irrevocably on October 23, 1983, my mother's birthday. I had driven to Rego Park, NY, where she lived to celebrate with her, having brought her a new Zenith color television set as her birthday present; for some years, she had resisted getting a color TV, saying that black-and-white was good enough for her. Of course, we found this silly, but respected her decision even if we did not agree with it.

Now that she was approaching the age of eighty, however, she was more and more home-bound. Therefore, a good, modern television set had become a real priority; and when I installed the new Zenith set and turned it on, it was gratifying when she looked at its multi-color clear picture and said that now she was sorry that she had put us off for so many years, as she loved it.

We went out to the nearby Sizzler Restaurant for lunch and then returned to my mother's apartment 3A, where she had lived since shortly after my father had died twenty years earlier. As I flipped on the TV to check out its reception one more time, I saw live coverage of the tragic truck bombing of the American Marine Barracks in Beirut, Lebanon. Early that morning, Beirut time, a Mercedes-Benz truck had driven to the Beirut International Airport where the Marines were housed, substituted for a hijacked water delivery truck which routinely visited that base. After turning onto an access road and circling a parking lot, the driver then accelerated and crashed through the barbed wire fence surrounding the parking lot, sped past two unprepared sentry posts, ran through a gate and straight into the lobby of the Marine headquarters, while the Marine guards were still getting their weapons loaded and shouldered.

The truck's driver, an early suicide bomber (that terror tactic was new, at the time), then detonated some twelve thousand pounds of TNT explosive, collapsing the four-story cinder-block building into rubble. According to news reports then and later, the force of the explosion lifted the building off its foundation, shearing off the concrete-supporting columns which were reinforced with steel rods. The massive building then fell in upon itself, with a ball of flaming gas generated by the explosive device, which was enhanced. There was a heavy shock wave and debris rained down in all directions. The entire event was a total nightmare – for the Marines, the nation, and particularly for someone whose warning fell on deaf ears and blind eyes in Washington!

This terror tragedy was preventable! It was the culmination of all of my fears, which began with Israeli General Chaim Yaron's dinner at Bradley airport near Hartford several months earlier. He had warned that this terrorist event was going to happen, and had even known the likely location of the target. He had predicted that it would occur fairly soon, as terrorists then were not known for their patience. The only thing he had not known was just when the atrocity would occur; now, sadly and tragically, that final question had been definitively answered, at the cost of several hundred Marine lives!

We learned a few minutes later that a similar suicide attack had occurred against the French peacekeepers' barracks about four miles away in the Ramlet al Baida section of West Beirut. Another bomber drove his truck down a ramp into that building's garage. The eight-story building was leveled to the ground. Ironically, part of the death toll there, fifty-eight French soldiers, resulted from the large number who had gathered on their balconies just before their own bombing, to see what was happening at the Beirut Airport as a result of the huge column of fire and smoke which had arisen there from the Marine Barracks bombing which had just occurred. These attacks had been cleverly coordinated.

In that first of those two bombings, two hundred and forty-one U.S. service members had lost their lives: two hundred twenty Marines, eighteen Naval personnel, and three Army soldiers. Sixty more Americans were injured. It was the deadliest single-day death toll for the United States Marine Corps since the World War II Battle of Iwo Jima, and was the deadliest single attack on Americans overseas since World War II. It was indeed a day of infamy for the world, as well as perhaps the beginning of a new brand of terrorism which has yet to be ended.

Therefore, after watching as much of the Beirut bombing coverage as we could stand, I said goodbye to my mother and left for Connecticut. The four-hour return drive seemed to take forever. What I had hoped would be a very happy birthday event in her honor had turned into a very sad occasion. In the aftermath of the Beirut Marine Barracks bombing, President Ronald Reagan and Defense Secretary Cap Weinberger said there would be no change in America's policy in Lebanon or in our participation in the peacekeeping effort. That theme was reiterated by U.S. Vice President George H. W. Bush, who toured the Marine bombing site on October 26 and said the United States "would not be cowed by terrorists." Cap the Knife let it be known, through "anonymous defense department sources," that he had privately opposed the stationing of our Marines in Lebanon.

Whether his opposition stemmed from the warning he had received from Hartford Congresswoman Barbara Kennelly was not known to anyone, and certainly not to me. But, in any event, he had shamefully done nothing about the warnings he had received.

The responses to the Beirut bombings were quite disparate. While the perpetrators were never totally identified, as several militant Shia groups claimed responsibility, the Free Islamic Revolutionary Movement provided names of the two suicide bombers.

Terrorists from the Hezbollah group were thought to have been involved, although that group did not proclaim its formal existence until 1985. Shortly after the bombings, the French retaliated by bombing Islamic Revolutionary Guard positions in the Beqaa Valley of Lebanon. President Reagan had planned on using special forces to target the Sheik Abdullah barracks in Baalbek, Lebanon, which housed the Iranian Revolutionary Guard forces believed to train the Hezbollah militants and terrorists. Caspar Weinberger, however, lobbied against that course of action, and the planned attack never occurred. There was indeed very little American direct response to the Beirut tragedy – but our Marines were moved offshore; then, in February, 1984, President Reagan ordered their withdrawal from Lebanon. The Marines were completely gone by the end of that February; the rest of the Multinational Peacekeeping Force was gone by April of 1984, which was indeed just what the terrorists wanted. We had lost.

Watching this entire tragic fiasco from the far-removed vantage of Connecticut, I had become quite depressed. These events in Lebanon had the air of a Greek tragedy; they were indeed not inevitable, not unavoidable, but had happened because of many blunders, misjudgments, and the human tendency to procrastinate. Over and over again, I paraded the entire sequence of incidents through my mind, from beginning to horrid end. What else might have been done, how could the tragedy have been avoided or prevented? It was essential to find answers, and to apply the Lessons of Lebanon before the next terror tragedy occurred.

CHAPTER TWENTY-SEVEN

◆

OLD BUSINESS

Meanwhile, life went on – and my professional life was serving as the Connecticut and Western Massachusetts Director for the Israeli Securities Agency. My duties covered nearly twenty communities throughout the area, and required sixty to eighty hours per week, since there were many evening and Sunday meetings besides the regular work-day. As time went by, the events of October 23, 1983 faded a bit. On the next October 23, my mother Anne Elander celebrated her 80th birthday; and frankly I did not think much about the Beirut tragedy on that same day one year earlier. Since her color television was working fine, I got her a different kind of 80th Birthday present: a unique handmade "tree of life" pendant or brooch, set in sterling silver with all sorts of precious gemstones. After that birthday, I never again saw her without that item of jewelry. She lived until mid-May of 1993, and was still wearing it then.

I had ceased any involvement with the Israeli Consulate in New York, and had not heard further from any staff there ever since our abortive meeting in the early fall of 1983. For some months afterwards, I waited for some apology for their implied threat; in retrospect, their defense attaché was probably waiting for my own apology for threatening to take the Beirut bombing story to the New York Times. However, no apology came in either direction, and I had decided that I should indeed have taken my secret information about the risks to our Marines to the New York Times as I had threatened to do. Perhaps the bombing might have been avoided – with some major publicity on the risk, Defense Secretary Weinberger would have had to act. At least, that was my theory, and so I began to take on myself responsibility for what had happened. Could I, should I, have done more? How would I ever know? The entire fiasco became a bit of an obsession to me.

It was therefore a bit of a relief when I received word of another piece of news, this time from the Chief of Staff to Congresswoman Barbara Kennelly. He had called me just before Thanksgiving of 1983 and asked me to stop by Barbara's office the next time I was in downtown Hartford. Naturally, I made it a point to be there the very next day, as I thought he might have news on the pending matter of a nuclear submarine for Israel, in exchange for Jacob Jacobson's badly-needed land adjacent to the Submarine Base. In that surmise, I was correct – but it was not the news I had hoped to hear.

Essentially, I was told that Defense Secretary Caspar Weinberger had refused our proposal; Cap the Knife had prevented any possibility of a nuclear submarine for Israel. The Representative's Chief of Staff had received a phone call from the Deputy Secretary of Defense with that bad news. No specific reason was given, simply "that it would not be in America's best interests to provide such equipment to Israel." Since I was not satisfied with this vague explanation, I called Barbara Kennelly to wish her a happy Thanksgiving that weekend. She replied, "And the same to you, Eugene. Let me guess: you have heard the news about the denial of a nuclear sub to Israel, which has also prompted your call, is that not the case?" I had to admit that to be true, and I asked Barbara if she could possibly find out more about why our proposal was denied. She replied, "I have anticipated you; Cap Weinberger is at his home in Avon, Connecticut, for the Thanksgiving holiday; he kept it when he left United Technologies for the Pentagon. We are to see him tomorrow, the day after Thanksgiving."

Although I had met Weinberger a couple of times at meetings before he went to the Pentagon, I had certainly never been to his palatial mansion in Hartford's upscale Avon suburb. Upon approaching the gate at the end of his long, curving driveway, I found U.S. Marines guarding it, just as they guard the approaches to the Naval Submarine Base in Groton. I had to show my passport and was then admitted to the estate, as the meeting was on Cap's approved schedule.

Another Marine took my car at the front door to the large, elegant house; a third searched me and then admitted me to a special audience room separate from the rest of the home. The Defense Secretary obviously kept his public and private lives separate. A few minutes later, Barbara Kennelly arrived, alone this time; apparently, her staff had the Thanksgiving weekend to themselves. We chatted until Cap Weinberger himself came into the room, accompanied by an aide. He was a handsome man of middle age, but I was struck by his icy gaze and stern lips; I wondered if he ever smiled, which he certainly did not do during our rather-brief meeting.

Barbara first introduced me as the regional director for the Israeli Securities Agency; Weinberger merely nodded at me, saying nothing. She then said that it was both Jacob Jacobson and I who had introduced the nuclear submarine request on behalf of the State of Israel, and that we were seeking more information as to why it had been declined, apparently by the Pentagon rather than by the Navy. I waited through an expectant pause, and then Cap the Knife said, "Had it not been for the Beirut bombing, Israel might well have received that submarine. The timing of that terror bombing was most unfortunate, in more ways than you can possibly know."

I had not yet said anything, but felt a need to respond to this cryptic statement. So, at that point, I interjected that we had left the matter in the capable hands of the United States Navy's top command, and had been unaware that it had come before Weinberger. He replied, "You are obviously not well versed in the ways of Washington. Any matter involving a foreign power, even such a close ally as Israel, must involve the State Department, the Defense Department, the National Security Council, the CIA and several other security agencies, and ultimately the President himself. Along the way, one or more of those agencies gave a negative response to the proposal which you and Jacob Jacobson made on behalf of the Israelis. That is all it would normally take to sink your proposal, if you will pardon the pun. But, on top of that, the President happens to be displeased with Israel at present – due to the Lebanon Marine Barracks bombing."

I felt, listening to this lecture from Cap Weinberger, that he thought me to be totally naïve about the ways of Washington, which indeed was true. But seeing that now there was nothing to lose, as the deal for the nuclear submarine was clearly dead in the water, I ventured this further comment, "In view of all those factors, Secretary Weinberger, I believe that the tragic bombing of the Marine Barracks in Beirut, of which you were warned in advance, must have played a major role in that negative determination on the nuclear sub for Israel. If President Reagan is displeased with Israel, it can only be because he was not given full and fair information on the facts of the bombing. Israel warned your officers in Lebanon that those Marines were at severe risk, and you yourself had advance warning as well. No real precautions were taken in spite of those warnings, resulting in so many unnecessary deaths of our brave troops. Now, the undeserved blame is being put on Israel. A 'fall guy' was needed, and found. Perhaps the President should know the full facts, not just your version of them."

As I was making these remarks, I felt Barbara Kennelly tapping my leg with her foot, undoubtedly to shut me up. I saw the aide to the Defense Secretary sort of freeze, while Cap the Knife got red in the face and began breathing hard. I was really angry, though, and not thinking of consequences – the first of those being the meeting's immediate end.

CHAPTER TWENTY-EIGHT

CONSEQUENCES

Barbara Kennelly and I were escorted at once out of the Weinberger home and to our vehicles; all Cap the Knife had had to do was to nod, and his aide closed the meeting. I had much respect for our good Congresswoman, and was waiting for her condemnation of my comments. Instead, she broke out laughing, shook my hand and said, "Eugene, you are both very brave and very foolhardy to talk to the Secretary of Defense that way. You are one of very few people who would dare to tell that SOB the truth. I wish I could give you my congratulations, but unfortunately you inadvertently made my own work harder. It will be a long time, and will take a lot of stroking, to re-establish relationships with Cap the Knife." Still smiling wistfully, she got into her car and drove off; I did the same, wondering what the consequences of all of this would be for me. It took some time to find out; and when I did, some of those consequences were quite unexpected.

What was really on my mind, however, was how I would break this disappointing news to Jacob Jacobson, who owned the land adjacent to the Groton Submarine Base, land which might have been exchanged for Israel's right to that nuclear submarine (Israel would still have been expected to pay for it, per the July meeting at the Sub Base). Thus, I made an appointment with Jacobson at once.

When we met at his office and I gave him a full report on the negative decision about the sub and the meeting with Caspar Weinberger, he leaned back and breathed a sigh. After a short pause, he said, "Well, of course I am disappointed, Eugene, although I knew all along that it was a long shot. We may never know if that nuclear submarine would have been provided to Israel had the Beirut bombing not occurred. But all that is moot – the bombing is a reality, and the sub is not. Now I will still offer my land to the Navy, but at the fair market price. I am, after all, a businessman, and I am fully prepared to do business with them. As a matter of fact, I have already secured a good piece of land further up Route 12 for my shopping center."

There were, however, further consequences for me as a result of the developments of those past few months, including two meetings which turned out to affect my life: the meeting with the Israeli defense attaché in New York, and the meeting with Caspar Weinberger at his home. I began to realize that my behavior at both meetings had involved strategic mistakes. I had "blown my cool," as the saying went; and losing full control of oneself is never a good thing. It may be enjoyable for the moment, but not for the longer term. Now, I came to think that I had made a fool of myself twice: first with the Israelis, and then with the Secretary of Defense.

Since there was nothing much I could do at that point to make amends, such as to apologize, without looking even more foolish, I chalked those mistakes up to human error. I decided to just get on with my life, but that same past was not going to let go of me so easily. Those consequences began with my next meeting in New York with the field staff director at the Israeli Securities Agency, a man widely disliked by the field staff whom he supervised. Joe Guttersnipe, as he was nicknamed, combined being nasty with not being overly bright; nevertheless, I had requested an urgent meeting with him.

I had learned that the ISA Boston office director, a young woman named Suzanne, had accepted a new position with a major Boston hospital. Having told Joe many months earlier that I wanted to apply for the Boston post should it become available, as it would be a major promotion, I used this next supervisory meeting to put in that application.

Joe sort of smirked then, asking me, "Eugene, do you think the Israeli Consulate here would endorse you for Boston?" I was totally surprised, as I had not known that my boss knew about my encounter with the Israeli defense attaché. While I was thinking about this, Joe added, "In case you are wondering, there are important people who consider you to be a troublemaker. You can forget about Boston; you started with us in Connecticut, and that is where you will stay, if you are lucky and coop-erative — no promotion for you."

Having learned my lesson about blowing up at meetings, I managed to stay calm, or at least appear so, at Joe's refusal to consider promot-ing me – ever. We then talked about some campaign matters, and I left the ISA headquarters, which by then had moved to Lexington Avenue in Midtown. On the street outside, I thought about going to the Israeli Consulate again – but I decided against doing so because it would change nothing about the fix I was in. I was now a pariah at ISA; since I did my job well, I would be retained, but never promoted. Therefore, I needed to make future plans realistically.

On the commuter train back to New Haven, to pick up my car and drive to Hartford, I kept thinking about the day's developments. Joe Guttersnipe had made the handwriting on the wall very clear; I was not going anywhere at ISA, despite outstanding campaign work, because of extraneous factors. One firm decision I made then and there was to get on with my life, with no regrets. I recalled the words of an official during the Nixon era:

"When the going gets tough, the tough get going." It was high time to consider options.

◆

LABOR OF LOVE

I have always believed that fate, karma, the Almighty, or whatever it is that guides human destinies has guided me. I had happened to note, in a newspaper classified ad, that Central Connecticut State University in New Britain needed a part-time economics lecturer for their Saturday morning classes. This was generally an unpopular time for faculty to teach, and I applied and was accepted. I might not be going to Boston for ISA, but I would be going to New Britain for CCSU. Since I had missed teaching, I looked forward to the position. I was scheduled to teach a Principles of Economics course beginning next semester, January 1984, half an hour from my modest home in Windsor.

Nor was CCSU my only new direction that January. The ISA had an organization of all of its regional directors around the United States; there were some forty of us at that time. In its early days, Israel was dominated by the Labor Party, which is very pro-union. Shortly after its founding in 1951, the Israeli Securities Agency had allowed its key staff to form an organization, the Professional Personnel Group or PPG, to represent us. Actually, under American labor laws, which ruled because ISA was an American corporation even if wholly owned by the Israeli Finance Ministry, ISA had had little choice in the matter of employee representation; the non-professional employees had a union too. Over the years, the PPG had maintained a certain amount of militancy as to pay, benefits, working conditions, and the like. A new PPG President was to be chosen at that time, as the former President had served out his term of office.

I had become active in the PPG upon taking over the Connecticut and Western Massachusetts ISA office. I believed that worker rights needed to be protected, and further believed that it was up to each ISA staff member to do his or her share of that vital protecting. When a vacancy occurred on the PPG Board, I was appointed to it by Alan, then our President. Being a labor economist, I handled grievances and helped to write the draft proposal for our next contract with ISA. In the late fall, I received a call from Alan at home, as we tried to keep PPG business out of the office and to use our own time for it. Alan told me, without ado, that the outgoing officers of the PPG wanted to nominate me for the Presidency. When I tried to say that I was not ready for the post, being a relative newcomer to ISA, Alan told me that actually I would be drafted for the PPG Presidency if I did not accept the nomination. Thus, I had little choice in the matter.

A Board meeting was scheduled for a Newark Airport hotel in December, only two weeks off, and I told Alan I would consider the matter and was willing to discuss it further at that meeting. At Newark I learned that two other PPG Board members with more seniority had accepted new positions, one of those being the outgoing Boston director, for whose job I had tried unsuccessfully to apply with Joe, my supervisor.

Several others on our small board had already served as President. The reality was that, of those remaining, I was the best choice because I had considerable knowledge of labor matters and was outspoken. The Board did not know that I had been too outspoken on occasion in the recent past, particularly with an Israeli official and also with Defense Secretary Weinberger. Had they known, it probably would have made no difference to their selection. I was nominated, and elected unanimously by the full PPG membership the following week. Now, unfortunately, I would have to work closely with the ISA field director, nicknamed Joe Guttersnipe, who had denied me any promotion at ISA, ever.

For the next few years, I did not focus on alerts, bombings, terrorism, and the like. Teaching Saturday morning classes at Central Connecticut State University was often enjoyable but more time-consuming that I had expected, as I found that there were many new developments in my field of economics; I had been somewhat out of touch. I had to be a student as well as a teacher, spending time each week catching up with my field.

I had also discovered that the Presidency of the PPG took far more time that I had expected. I complained to Alan, the former President and now a Board Member, that he had not told me just how much "hand holding" was required by our membership, who were often experiencing professional, or even personal, problems. Alan laughed and said, "Eugene, had I told you about all that, you might have refused to take the job. When I was nominated for the same post four years earlier, nobody told me either."

We were entering a period of intensive negotiations with ISA, as our labor contract expired at the end of the first year of my term of office. It took months to draw up a new contract proposal calling for five percent wage increases in each of the next three years, the most we had ever asked, as I had done a survey and found that we regional directors were grossly underpaid compared to the earnings of comparable executives. ISA tried to use Israel's financial problems against us, telling us how tough things were in that fledgling nation, and how we should be "patriotic" and just ask for token raises. This was a philosophy which I rejected out-of-hand, as I had managed to find out what ISA's top national executives earned – they were not being asked to make the same sacrifices which they now asked of us PPG members.

Negotiations began in September of 1985, continuing right up to New Year's Eve. The five percent annual salary increase was the major sticking point, and I knew that we needed to have a breakthrough before the old contract expired at midnight. So I decided on a two-pronged strategy: first, we called a strike for New Year's Day, calling each of our forty-plus members from the Summit Hotel in New York, where we were staying, and getting a reluctant majority vote for that strike – reluctant because we would not be paid during it. The second prong of the strategy was to leak to a friend of mine at the New York Times that the Professional Personnel Group had called a strike for New Year's Day, and that we would be picketing the ISA national office in New York starting immediately upon the commencement of the strike.

I then called the ISA Human Resources Director, to notify him that we were going out on strike the next day unless the new contract was signed, sealed, and delivered on New Year's Eve. My contact at the New York Times, meanwhile, called the new president of ISA, a former Israeli Ambassador who had replaced The General, to check the validity of my news leak of the strike and the picketing, not only in New York but outside all ISA offices around the country. Literally at the eleventh hour, eleven p.m. December 31, ISA called an emergency negotiating session and yielded on the five percent annual raise and several of our other demands. Over the next three contract years, our pay went up by fifteen percent, to approach the remuneration of comparable jobs at other agencies.

When we all shook hands after the completion of negotiations, the human resources director, who had replaced Nate upon the latter's retirement, said to me, "Eugene, you and your gang have stolen the store." I thanked him for the compliment to the PPG, although of course he did not mean it that way. I was to discover, however, that there was a price to be paid for union leadership, regardless of its being for a worthy cause.

CHAPTER TWENTY NINE

◆

REFUSAL

The nature of that price became clear only when I retired from the PPG Presidency after having served for two terms, a total of four years and the limit under our bylaws. My successor was the Vice President, while I retired to just being on the board again. Those four years of union leadership had been very satisfying, and I had also become active with AFSCME, the American Federation of State, County, and Municipal Employees, our parent union. I continued as a delegate to their District Council 1707, representing all New York City area AFSCME units.

What I had not fully realized was that, as reigning President of the APP, I had been somewhat protected from the malice of Joe, ISA's National Field Director. Harassing of union presidents is not generally a good idea, as it is prohibited by both Federal and State legislation. The same cannot be said for harassing union ex-presidents, however; and Joe came after me with pent-up vengeance which proved that he had the backing of the new ISA President, known as The Ambassador, who had replaced my friend The General.

The Ambassador had never liked me, and the feeling was mutual. The Israelis had given him the post as a political plum; but whereas The General was an admirable and competent leader, The Ambassador was a pompous blowhard who told insiders he had been banished to ISA due to Israeli politics, believing that he deserved a much better post. Rumor had it that he had wanted to become Israeli Ambassador to the United

Nations, a post he was denied. He was therefore not a "happy camper", and he managed to make most of the key ISA staff unhappy also.

Thus, we had to hear over and over, at every staff meeting, about his work on the Camp David Accords which had led to a peace-of-sorts between Israel and Egypt in 1978. President Jimmy Carter had brokered this good-faith agreement, but the peace was a cold one at best. Still, a cold peace is always preferable to a hot war, and Egypt was no longer likely to attack Israel as it had several times in the past. But The Ambassador took more credit than was due him; it was Israel's Menachem Begin and Egypt's Anwar Sadat who worked so long and hard at Camp David, with President Jimmy Carter, to achieve the peace agreement – it was not the result of the efforts of ISA's puffed-up blowhard.

Now, as only a former PPG President, I no longer had the same level of union job protection. While Joe and ISA did nothing overt, there was continuous and escalating pressure on me to sell more Israeli securities, hold more programs, stage more dinners, and so on. The handwriting on the wall had become obvious, and I began to consider career alternatives.

Then matters came to a head when I got a call from The Ambassador himself, a rather unusual occurrence and one which I suspected would not contain good news. Without any preamble, the Ambassador (he insisted on that title, even though it no longer applied) told me, "You are directed to stage a major tribute dinner for former American Defense Secretary Caspar Weinberger next fall; I will be the major and keynote speaker at the event." He then hung up without even giving me the courtesy of a reply – which was just as well, as I knew immediately that I would not follow his direct order, that I would never honor Cap the Knife, the man who had let those Marines in Beirut remain at risk even after he was repeatedly warned of the danger to them. Hell would have to freeze over before any such dinner took place in Connecticut, where Weinberger had reassumed his duties as United Technologies CEO after President Ronald Reagan left office and Cap the Knife left the post of Reagan's Defense Secretary.

My technique for avoiding the Ambassador's command was, first, that of fogging. I simply took no action towards a tribute dinner for Cap the Knife, ignoring the matter. No tribute committee was established, which would normally be the first step in the process, as many business and governmental leaders in Connecticut and beyond would want their names on dinner and pre-dinner invitations, no matter how they felt about the honoree. It would be smart politics and good business to be on the tribute list; the Republicans were still in power, now under President George H. W. Bush, and there would have been no problem putting together a successful dinner honoring the former Secretary of Defense -- except that it was never going to happen in Connecticut.

After a month or so, however, fogging ceased to work, as my immediate boss, Joe, called me from New York to ask how the "Weinberger Tribute Dinner" was coming. I enjoyed immensely asking Joe, "What dinner are you talking about?," playing innocent.

Joe's voice then took on an edge, as he said, "The dinner The Ambassador ordered you to produce, with him as the featured speaker. I have checked and no date was cleared with his office. Why are you sitting on your hands, Eugene?" (That last comment was one of Joe's favorite expressions, so much so that the PPG had once staged a mini-play at a union meeting, in which I played "Joe Guttersnipe" and used that phrase repeatedly.)

Knowing that it was only a matter of time – and not too much time, at that – before I would hear from The Ambassador on this matter, I had my response ready – a response he would not like at all. Thus, I then said, "Joe, I may be old fashioned, but I have always believed that any dinner honoree must be honorable, or the event has no credibility. You have never met or been involved with Weinberger, but I have, as has our Congresswoman, Barbara Kennelly, and many others here in Connecticut. He is soundly disliked here, for cutting thousands of jobs at United Technologies while paying himself and his board exorbitant salaries. But far worse, he has refused to support the State of Israel in endless ways, and he knowingly endangered the Marine Barracks in Beirut, which resulted in the loss of over two hundred forty lives. There will be no dinner for Cap the Knife staged by my office, not now, not ever." I then hung up the phone before he could respond, just as the Ambassador had done to me. Of course, I knew that would not be the end of the matter, nor was it. The fight had only begun.

The next development in the non-event for Weinberger was a call from Joe's boss, the legendary nearly-retired Executive Vice President of ISA. Morris had been among the first employees of the Israeli Securities Agency, starting in 1951 shortly after it was founded. He did not normally get involved in such local matters as this one; in fact, many of us field staff wondered what he actually did do at ISA; but then he was moving towards retirement and perhaps had earned the right to take things a bit easier. He was not, however, taking my refusal to do this tribute dinner easier; he was incensed, and shouted at me on the phone for some minutes, long enough that I put the phone down on my desk and waited for his tirade to cease.

When I finally heard silence on the phone, I picked it up again just as Morris was saying, "Well?" I replied, infuriatingly, that I would make no response to such an angry outburst, and that should he wish to ask me any questions or make any comments, he needed to put them in writing, so that I could share them with my attorneys. Morris then screamed again, over me, "What attorneys, you SOB?" Actually, I had no attorneys, had never even thought of needing them, but it just seemed like such a golden opportunity to twist his tail that I could not resist – nor could I resist hanging up at that point, either.

I made a bet with myself that the next call would be from the firm's president and CEO, The Ambassador, but I was wrong. Instead, at 11 a.m. the next day, a delegation from the ISA National Office in New York walked into my office in West Hartford. The delegation included our Big Three, The Ambassador himself along with Joe and Morris, plus our legal director. They demanded an immediate meeting, and we went across the hall to our conference room where I closed the door. Then they let me have it, starting with The Ambassador – all of them ranting, raving, raging, threatening, and generally having major temper tantrums. I let them get it out of their systems, while wondering if my staff were going to call the police due to all the noise and commotion.

When they finally ran down, after about half an hour, I said very calmly, "The tone and content of your remarks are both totally unacceptable. I have given my objections to this event to both Joe and Morris, and I am sure that they have shared those objections with The Ambassador. You all fully understand my position, that here in Connecticut we will honor only the honorable. Cap the Knife does not fall into that category, and will not be honored here; if you choose to honor him in New York, that is your affair. But should you attempt further pressure or try to take over my office to stage this dinner, or should you try to fire me for my refusal to conduct it, I will be in the offices of the Hartford Courant newspaper and of all the TV and radio stations the very next day. And, the day after that, I will visit The New York Times, and then The Washington Post, and so on. Nor will the Jerusalem Post and other Israeli newspapers be ignored. Believe it."

With that said, I got up, left the conference room to their astounded expressions, and returned to my office across the hall. After about fifteen minutes, Joe came in alone, and said to me, "We are returning to New York, but you have not heard the last of this. You have no understanding of those with whom you are dealing; you will pay a heavy price for your stubbornness."

When he had finished and was turning to leave, I touched a switch on my IBM mini-recorder, which I used for meetings and making notes to myself while traveling, playing back the tirade from the conference room, starting with the Ambassador, and then fast forwarding to the threat Joe had just made. Then I said, "This meeting is now on the record. Have a safe trip back to New York. Shalom!"

While I had made a brave front during the visit of the major delegation from ISA headquarters, I also realized that my ISA bridges had been burned with finality. That burning process had undoubtedly begun with the Israeli military attaché's negative report on my brash reaction to his implied threat, if I had had the temerity to expose the risks to our Marines in Lebanon. The process continued through my four years as President of the Professional Personnel Group, when our success at securing salaries more in line with those at comparable firms was viewed by ISA as some form of disloyalty to the cause, whatever that cause might be. Now, the final shoe had fallen (perhaps more shoes than I had legs); I had successfully blocked any tribute dinner for former President Ronald Reagan's defense secretary, Cap the Knife. My fate was sealed, and while I would probably continue at ISA for some time, the powers-that-be were out to get me, and eventually they would succeed. My days there were numbered; it was time to move on.

Therefore, at once, I began circulating my resume to various securities firms, colleges and universities, and social agencies in the greater Hartford area. I did not want to leave that area, as I was still Saturday morning economics teacher at Central Connecticut State University. Meanwhile, I continued at ISA, with successful tribute dinners for regional government officials, business leaders, and humanitarians, all of whom deserved their honors, unlike the proposed honoree at the dinner which I had refused to organize.

One of my proudest volunteer achievements was establishing the Hartford State Technical College Foundation. I had been approached by an acquaintance who worked at the College, and who invited me to visit there, to see what they were doing, primarily for inner city youth. This small two-year institution was literally saving lives, getting teens and post-teens to give up using and dealing drugs in favor of becoming technicians, legal and medical assistants, computer information specialists, and the like. The Foundation was set up to provide that "extra edge of excellence," a phrase I had coined to include acquiring more library books, computers and software, lab equipment, and whatever else was needed. I continued as Foundation President until the HSTC was merged into the area community college system, by Legislative decision, and the Foundation merged also.

CHAPTER THIRTY

◆

RETURN TO ISRAEL

It may seem ironic, after all the commotion I had stirred up at the Israeli Securities Agency, which they undoubtedly considered to be insubordination, by refusing to do a tribute dinner for Caspar Weinberger, that I was invited on a Mission to Israel once more. However, in the union agreement which ISA despised, we had continued the clause providing that all key staff went to Israel once every five years, at company expense. Upon receiving the invitation for the Summer 1992 mission, I then informed ISA's travel department, still headed by the legendary Mr. Israel, that I would indeed participate; Mr. Israel then informed me that I would be the Mission Leader, having been on several previous Missions. I suspected that this "honor" was actually punishment for my ISA "transgressions," as the Mission Leader had a host of unpleasant responsibilities.

As I prepared for our June departure, planning on visiting my mother in Rego Park, New York on the way to JFK Airport, I got a bright idea about how to pay for all those Mission incidentals added to make up for a part of trip's costs; I went to my safe deposit box and took out some of the State of Israel securities I had been accumulating since I had begun working for ISA ten years earlier. Some of the Bonds had already matured, but I had not been in a rush to cash them; others had an early redemption provision which I could utilize in Israel. Those Bonds would provide needed spending money, and I even acquired a "money belt" with an inside zipper compartment to hold them. While that belt accentuated my middle-aged spread, the added security for the Securities was worth it.

Upon arriving at Ben Gurion Airport on a Sunday in late June, 1992, I went to the Jerusalem Hilton once again, and I told the concierge that I had some securities to cash. The next morning, he directed me to the nearest branch of Bank Leumi, the major Israeli financial institution, where I turned in the Bonds and received their cash value in Israeli shekels. I had taken a calculator with me, and I double checked that the amount was correct, then asked, "What about the U.S. tax withholding?" The head teller, with whom I was dealing, replied, "This is Israel. We are not responsible for U.S. tax withholding. It is your choice as to whether or not you report interest earned on your Bonds; that is not our concern."

It may seem strange that this American income tax issue had never occurred to me; but my office was in Connecticut, not Israel, and there we took the U.S. tax laws very seriously. The American bank which serviced our securities was responsible for issuing tax forms for any Bonds redeemed or cashed in at any of our offices, including the New York headquarters. Failure to report such interest was a Federal crime on the parts of both ISA, the issuer of the Bonds, and of the recipient holding them. So, my concern seemed to center on those Bonds cashed in Israel, and I did a quick mental calculation, resulting in a rough estimate that some half billion dollars of Israeli debt securities would have been cashed in, in Israel, since the 1950s, of which nearly two-thirds would have been redeemed by Americans.

Now, I was determined to find out how the necessary tax reporting on those Bonds' interest had been handled in Israel. Since most of that Mission's sightseeing was quite similar to what had occurred on my first trip to Israel some years earlier, I skipped the Mission's first day, when Jerusalem would be toured. Walking to the Jerusalem ISA office, which I had visited on my previous trips to Israel, I thought about how I would broach this sensitive issue to their controller, who was in charge of redemption matters, both of matured Bonds and those with early redemption privileges. I had phoned Avram, the controller, to tell him that I was coming to discuss a sensitive matter, and he met me at the office door, introduced me around to the staff, and then escorted me to his office.

Avram then asked me what was on my mind, and I told him about my experience at Bank Leumi, cashing in some Bonds without any tax withholding. Then, with my hat as an economist figuratively on my head, I asked him if that was consistent with tax treaties between Israel and the United States. It had been my understanding that, under those long-standing treaties, each nation agreed to give full faith and credit to the tax laws of the other nation, so that there was full reciprocity. That would seem to me to require full tax reporting by Bank Leumi and any other institution cashing Americans' securities in Israel, just as our American bank performed such reporting for ISA Bonds cashed in the United States.

Avram was an Orthodox Jew, which could be determined by his wearing a kipa, a small round covering on the back of his head. He had a substantial black beard and was an imposing figure, as he leaned forward, shook his index finger in my face, and said, "Eugene, I have already heard about you from The Ambassador and others at ISA. You have a bad habit of sticking your nose where it is not wanted. In this case, that habit needs to be curbed at once. I understand that there is an American saying: 'Ask me no questions and I'll tell you no lies.' And, in this matter, I will tell you nothing." The meeting was clearly over, and I got up and left, returning to the Mission, which was then visiting the Knesset, the Israeli parliament, with its magnificent Chagall windows.

Since the remainder of our mission to Israel was quite similar to the public part of my previous trip, I will skip over the standard tourist attractions. We did visit some different sites, though. We saw an archeological dig near the Negev desert, where an ancient Roman city was being excavated; the archeologists were being assisted by a friend of mine named Arnie, who taught at the University of Connecticut, specializing in such historical research. We also saw the Crusader fortress at Acre, with its six-foot-thick walls, which had been nearly destroyed when the

Crusaders were thrown out of the Holy Land by its Muslim inhabitants under their great general, Saladin. We saw the museum housing the Dead Sea Scrolls, found by a shepherd boy some years before, in caves in the high cliffs near En Gedi where they had been preserved for two thousand years. These Scrolls documented many biblical events, and were unique and priceless.

It was really impressive to participate in many special events planned for us, such as a visit to a new power plant funded via investment funds ISA raised all over the world. While I also enjoyed these sites and activities, the matter of U.S. tax evasion kept bothering me. I raised it confidentially with some of my colleagues on the Mission, finding that the degree of knowledge among them varied.

Most had given little thought to the concern; in fact, some had been cashing securities in Israel for years without worrying about American tax liability on the interest. The few who had thought about the matter said that they preferred not to raise it; my old friend Ruby, from Florida, was again on this mission, his last before retirement. He had been on my first trip to Israel also, and he simply said, "Eugene, let sleeping dogs lie!" But in good conscience, I could not heed his advice. I had a feeling that this particular dog was due to awake in the near future, to Israel's disadvantage, due to its apparent complicity. So I answered Ruby with another proverb, saying, "Well, forewarned is truly forearmed."

CHAPTER THIRTY-TWO

◆

ULTIMATUM

I had spent a very enjoyable two weeks in Israel, returning safely to Connecticut in early July of 1992. I stopped at my mother's apartment on the way home, to deliver some gifts we had brought back for her. She had been in Israel several times in its early days, during the 1960s, stopping at a kibbutz or collective farm which specialized in footwear. Anne had "hammer toes" and it was very hard for her to find comfortable shoes, so when I visited that same kibbutz, I got her a pair of those special sandals there.

For my entire life, I have always had trouble just letting something go; sometimes I thought that I should have gotten therapy to learn how to drop matters which needed dropping, but had never done so. Therefore, the matter of the non-reporting of taxes on interest paid when ISA Bonds were cashed in Israel continued to bother me. Knowing that I would find out nothing from my boss, I developed a strategy in order to get answers.

ISA now had a new President, another General, as The Ambassador had returned to Israel once his term of appointment was finally over. That was good for me, as this new President as yet had nothing against me, unlike The Ambassador – and I wanted to keep it that way. So, I decided to approach the ISA legal director tactfully, regarding the "tax issue", on my next visit to New York. We had a Staff Conference every fall, to get us geared up to do our utmost, and I sought out our 'legal eagle' on a conference break and asked to speak with her privately.

We went into a small, vacant conference room, and she asked me, jokingly, "Are you ready to do that dinner now?" I knew she was referring to my refusal to honor Cap the Knife, the former American defense secretary; and I thought of a snappy comment but refrained. Instead, I told her, "I brought some matured ISA Bonds to Israel to cash there, along with a few that allowed early redemption. When I turned all of them in to Bank Leumi, I received the full proceeds, with no tax withholding, nor was I given a 1099 or other IRS form. That led me to approach our Controller in Jerusalem, who practically threw me out of his office when I asked about this matter. What gives?"

I was surprised that our top attorney seemed unsurprised by my question; instead, she gave me a long look and said, "You must be unaware that Avram, our Controller in Israel, called me after your visit. He was very angry, and asked me why you were poking around in what does not concern you. I told him I would discuss this with you upon your return, as we are now doing. Are you raising this as payback for our denying the Boston post to you? If so, you are not as smart as we both think that you are, as it will backfire."

At that time, I considered this head attorney, if not a friend, at least an associate and colleague. She had also been involved in ISA/PPG labor negotiations, and I had found her the most fair of the ISA team – much fairer than The Ambassador or Joe or their overpaid outside labor attorney. So I said, "Andrea, this is not some kind of ploy, nor is it any attempt to get back at ISA in some way. Rather, I am sincerely concerned that I might be working for a worldwide Israel-based firm which allows or even encourages avoidance of American income taxes. Not only is that despicable, as it violates the basic trust and honesty essential between two close allies – but it also is likely to be exposed at some point. Some investigative journalists, perhaps the Sixty Minutes television program or a leading newspaper, will get on to this sooner or later. Some editor will cash our securities in Israel and find the same result which I found, namely that no tax is withheld. It is even hinted to Bondholders that they need not pay American taxes. Is it ISA policy to turn our customers, often unknowingly, into tax cheats or worse?"

There was a long pause, and then she replied, "Eugene, this policy has continued since ISA was founded in 1951 and the first securities, ten-year Bonds, thus came due in 1961. That is more than thirty years ago. Meanwhile, our Bonds are no longer savings bonds; they are all current income securities, paying interest by check each year rather than accumulating. There is no useful purpose served by raising this matter now; it is on its way to becoming ancient history. Let it rest!"

I took that as her admission that my surmises were correct, that ISA had encouraged or ignored tax avoidance virtually since its inception. That was not something which anyone with a conscience could let rest. But I said nothing of that to our legal director, merely thanking her for the explanation. Again, I had much which I needed to consider.

Before this fall staff meeting adjourned, my supervisor, Joe "Guttersnipe", National Field Director, told me that he wanted to see me privately. When we met in his hotel room, the tax matter did not arise. Instead, Joe berated me for some ten minutes over not having raised more money that year. While it was true that my campaign was down, so was the economy in my entire area. The high-flying 1980s were gone, and I had tried numerous techniques to raise sales and help customers who were no longer in a position to invest with us. One of the top real estate developers in Hartford, Colonial Realty, had gone bankrupt recently, and one partner had even committed suicide. When Joe stopped his tirade, I mentioned some of these facts, inviting him to visit our West Hartford office to meet with our leadership. Joe replied, "Eugene, our last visit to your office, when you turned down the tribute dinner for Caspar Weinberger, was not very productive. It is up to you to solve your problems, that is not the role of the national office. You had better solve them very soon."

This time, I kept my temper and made no response. But, once more, I could see that ISA would continue to pressure me, with that pressure intensifying into harassment. I had seen this done to other regional directors, some of whom had called me as the PPG president to complain about it. Now that my second term as PPG president had expired, I knew I would be fair game for Joe and his management team to try to pick off. I needed to act before then – and so I did, but in a manner which surprised everyone at ISA.

Returning to Connecticut after the staff conference, I determined on a course of action, in view of all of the facts which I had ascertained, both in Israel and America. Now that "the cat was out of the bag" on the tax issue, I planned on notifying ISA, by certified mail, that American tax laws must be fully observed and implemented by the Israeli Securities Agency. I did not feel that I needed to clear this communication with the PPG Board for two reasons: first, I was merely telling ISA that the firm needed to follow U.S. tax laws as an American corporation, albeit with Israeli ownership; and second, that ISA had made clear that they wanted tax issues kept confidential. I sent confidential copies of my certified letter to our new union President, and to an old friend for safe-keeping.

That new PPG President called me the instant he received this communication; I had not previously talked to anyone about tax concerns, beyond our Controller in Israel and our legal director in New York. After the PPG leader expressed puzzlement, asking me what this was all about, I gave him a full briefing on the issue of ISA's non-withholding and non-reporting of U.S. taxes on securities cashed in Israel. There was a long pause, following which he said that he had never thought about that matter, it had never crossed his mind that the firm would violate U.S. tax laws in that manner. Then he added, "If this gets out to the news media or the public, all of us are in trouble. All Hell is going to break loose. I suppose that I am glad you are the one to have raised the matter, as your common sense helps protect our membership should it become public."

After a few more days, I got a call from the ISA legal head. She had received my letter regarding ISA tax policies, and had discussed the issue with the major New York bank which had handled and serviced our securities since 1951. The legend went that David Ben Gurion, the first Prime Minister of Israel, had chosen this particular bank for that purpose through a deal with the family which controlled the bank. The legal director said, in a very cold voice, "ISA and our Registrar Bank did not appreciate your letter; I warned you not to stir things up."

Expecting such a reaction, I had thought out my answer, which was, "You and I have always had a cordial professional relationship, based on mutual trust and respect. In that spirit, I am informing you that it is unconscionable for ISA to deprive the United States, its host nation here, of substantial tax revenues, presumably in order to sell more of its securities. Such a policy is intolerable, it is shocking, and it is also consummately stupid. When this comes out – and it will, sooner or later, without my involvement – ISA will have given the State of Israel a terrible black eye. All of our many enemies will have a field day over this. It will fan the flames of anti-Semitism, as word is spread that the Jewish state feels free to avoid its tax obligations to the United States, making American Jews appear disloyal, or worse. It is too bad if ISA's executives, and top Israeli Finance Ministry officials who ultimately are responsible for this agency, cannot see those truths – but I can and do. Tell those in power that they have three months to devise a plan to end this pernicious tax avoidance, and to present that plan to me. This is your sole opportunity to make the change internally. If that plan is not developed by the end of this year, I will go public as a whistle blower against ISA. The choice is yours, and that of your colleagues; make a wise one."

I hung up the phone then, as I doubted any further discussion at that point would be useful. It rang again later that morning, and it was The (New) General, our new National President, whom I had met only once, at the September staff conference. He had the reputation of being a hard man, but a fair one. I found the first of those reputations to be well-deserved, but not the second, as he stated, "I am not calling to discuss this tax matter with you; I am calling to tell you that, if you pursue it in any further way, either internally or externally, you will be terminated at once from our employment. Do I make myself clear?" I replied, "Yes, General, you are most clear, and I will be equally clear with you. ISA has three months to respond internally with a specific plan to correct the firm's abuse of American tax laws. That is pursuant to the certified letter I sent to ISA. Should that internal response not be forthcoming by the end of 1992, the tax issue, and perhaps others, will go to the American government, starting with the Internal Revenue Service and the Securities and Exchange Commission, which regulates ISA as a securities firm. Do I make myself clear, General?" I waited for his response, but there was only silence on the line.

The next reaction, however, came in a form I had not expected. I had attended an evening meeting of the Greater Hartford Community Relations Committee, of which I had been a member since moving to Connecticut. The Committee handled a wide range of community issues: religious, racial, governmental, and so on. Pulling out of the parking lot of the downtown church where the meeting was held, I had a feeling of being followed. By then I had purchased a Chrysler mini-limousine once belonging to Chrysler CEO Lee Iacocca, which I had restored, as they were no longer made. I pulled into a gas station on the way home, and a black Ford pulled in at the gas pump behind me, while a large man whom I had never seen before got out. Then I noticed that the Ford had U.S. diplomatic license plates, easy to distinguish by their red, white and blue format, which did not identify the nation to which the car was registered.

I knew that nation, though – it had to be the diplomatic vehicle of an Israeli, probably a Mossad agent posing as a Consular official, but one I had never met before. He said nothing to me, but after sitting in the gasoline lane while I filled up, not getting any gas himself, he pulled out behind me and began to follow me through the darkened Hartford streets. I shut off all lights on my Chrysler and, knowing the downtown area very well, screamed around corners and down back streets like a scene from a car chase in a B movie. I was not sure whether to hope the police spotted me, so that I could report his pursuit, or just hope to get away. The latter occurred; I managed to shake off the Ford and the Israeli agent. But I knew that I had been warned. I also knew that I was probably playing with fire, and might well get burned. I took the car chase as merely a warning. I believed that I was being told to go no further with the tax matter, and for the next three months, I did not follow up on my letter to ISA in any way. The ball was in their court, and I awaited their response by year-end. Meanwhile, I made my own future plans.

CHAPTER THIRTY-THREE

◆

WINDS OF CHANGE

It had become clear that I was unlikely to find suitable employment in my area of Connecticut. I did not want another job in the securities industry, which was in a state of decline in Connecticut due to the economic downturn. At that point, I was in my fifties, had not taught full-time for decades, and had become known as rather a troublemaker. This latter reputation was not due to any ISA affair, but rather because I was quite active in civic and political matters. As a lifelong Democrat, I was a volunteer economist for Bill Clinton, who had run successfully for President of the United States in 1991, taking office the following year. I had even met him twice, once in Hartford and later in Cromwell, Connecticut. I was very impressed with that highly-intelligent man, and with his charming wife Hillary, leading me to volunteer as an economist with his campaign.

Because I was also a board member of the Hartford Area Business Economists, I happened to comment at a luncheon meeting of HABE that I had found an "error" in the economic growth figures which then-President George H. W. Bush was presenting, during his run for a second term. Those figures were overstated by nearly one percent, perhaps not a big error but large enough to make it appear that the United States economic growth rate was increasing thanks to Bush, when in truth it was falling.

Little did I know that a reporter for the Hartford Courant newspaper was present at the HABE luncheon – at least not until the following morning when the front page of the Courant business section read: ECONOMIST CLAIMS BUSH FAKES GROWTH FIGURES.

When I called the Courant business editor to try to make clear that the headline was inaccurate, or at least overstated, he merely asked me if the story itself was correct. I had to confess that it was. He then gave me a lecture about headlines, mostly that they had to fit the available space and did not always accurately reflect the underlying story. The Courant would not run a correction. Then I found, all of a sudden, that some of my Republican business associates did not want to grant requests for appointments or meetings. I had offended the powerful.

It was another incident, though, which caused me to give up on finding suitable full-time employment in the Hartford area. After what seemed like endless application letters, I finally secured an interview with an "economics consulting firm." The ad for the job used a post office box number without identifying the employer, but they did invite me to come in for an interview. Still in the dark about this mysterious firm, I went to their address along Farmington Avenue in Hartford, going up in the elevator to the third floor. I had not checked the directory of offices, as I assumed the firm name would be on the office door upstairs – but I was wrong, the elevator opened onto a floor-size office divided into small modular cubicles.

Since I still did not know to whom I was applying, I went to the receptionist's desk and introduced myself, stating that I had an appointment with the human resources head. Then, with some embarrassment, I asked, "By the way, what is the name of this firm?" The receptionist gave me a strange look, and then said, pronouncing the words slowly and distinctly so that I would be sure to understand each and every one, "This is the Connecticut Business and Industry Association." Now, as I looked around with that new information, I saw that all of the staff were about twenty years younger than me, and each and every one wore suspenders, except for the few women. I even recognized a few from Hartford Area Business Economists meetings, as some were members of HABE.

The problem, however, was not merely my age and lack of suspenders. The real problem was that I had often taken stands against leaders of CBIA, a pro-business lobby which frequently fudged the economic facts to make a case for taking away vital rules and regulations imposed by the State upon CBIA members. I was amazed that I was even being interviewed, as I would not work for CBIA under any circumstances, nor would they want me to be there. That was the last straw in my Connecticut job search, perhaps the straw that broke the figurative camel's back. I needed to seek work elsewhere; the winds of change were blowing once more, hopefully in some sensible direction for my future.

CHAPTER THIRTY-FOUR

SECURITY DETAIL

While working and waiting to find the right opportunity, my time at ISA was winding down, and meanwhile my supervisor, Joe, continued to find ways to harass me. I had given ISA a three-month window of opportunity to mend its ways and to correct any violations of American tax and securities laws. I suspected that ISA's failure to collect taxes on debt securities cashed in Israel was not their only violation; there had been rumors around the national office of money laundering and other darker violations. Hence, I was not surprised to receive a faxed notice from Joe (who now hated to speak with me) ordering that I work a security detail for the upcoming visit of the new Israeli Prime Minister, Yitzhak Rabin, who had been elected to that post earlier that year.

For many years, I had done security work for ISA at such events as the annual Salute to Israel parade early each June in New York City. Prior to each parade, I would spend a few days in New York, being trained in various security techniques, mostly various forms of watchfulness which are taken for granted in Israel. There, if one sees a suspicious bag or package, or questionable behavior, or simply anything which seems out of place, one takes immediate steps to deal with the situation. If it appears to be more than one can handle personally, there are special ways of reaching those who can deal with problems.

My typical assignment was to watch doorways, alleys, windows, and rooftops as the parade wound its way up Fifth Avenue. I was given a radio headset, so that I could report any problems at once. On several occasions, I had done so, and luckily in all such cases, the situation had proven to be a false alarm. Most such security problems turned out to be false alarms, but Israelis take no chances. On my several Missions to Israel, I received further training, taking some responsibility for the safety of our delegation during the trip.

Once, in Bethlehem, on the West Bank of the Jordan River and therefore considered to be at risk, rocks had rained down on the roof of our bus, and I called in the military defense unit which patrolled that area to seek the perpetrators. On another occasion, we had to change our route to Eilat in the far South of Israel because of warnings of trouble along the regular road to that port city.

Then, in the late fall of 1992, I was commanded to join the security force protecting Prime Minister Rabin on his first visit to the United States in his new capacity. Yitzhak Rabin had been the head of the Israeli Labor Party for many years, and that party had taken over the government from the hawkish Likud party and its partners. I had met Rabin previously, both in Israel and in the United States. He was an imposing man, now in his 70s, a founder of the State of Israel going back to the era of the British occupation, and a leader for decades. His fondest dream was of peace between Jews and Arabs, and he had worked ceaselessly to achieve that difficult goal. Therefore, although Joe, my supervisor, considered the assignment to be an annoyance to me, I considered it to be a great privilege.

My particular responsibility was to work security at a major national luncheon for the Prime Minister at the Waldorf Astoria Hotel. New York's top political, civic, media, and social leadership were invited to the event, along with the heaviest of ISA's 'heavy hitters" who invested tens or even hundreds of thousands of dollars a year in our Bond securities. I would watch all entrants to the hotel elevators in advance of the luncheon, and then stand in the wings during the luncheon itself, watching the full crowd for any suspicious actions. My radio headset would provide instant access to those Israeli and American agents who would take further action, if necessary. Hopefully, I would merely get tired of standing before, during, and after the event. Nothing dangerous would occur.

On that particular day, though, good planning and good luck were not with us. While some of the guests were known to me from my many years with ISA, not all of them were, particularly those from outside of the greater New York area and those invited for political and similar reasons. Watching the Waldorf elevator to which I was assigned, I noted a middle-aged man with a swarthy complexion carrying a briefcase. I could tell from the floor indicator that the elevator stopped at the top floor of the Waldorf, on which the Rabin luncheon was being held. Something did not seem quite right about this man and his briefcase, something I could not pin down sufficiently to radio to the security detail supervisors. Therefore, I told my co-watcher that I needed to go up to the top floor on a security matter and he agreed to watch the elevator by himself until I returned. Upon exiting the elevator, I came to the registration table, where Joe, my supervisor, was among those key ISA staffers greeting the invited guests and checking off their names.

I also noticed that the same briefcase I had seen being carried onto the elevator in the lobby was now sitting, mostly hidden behind the drapes, on a windowsill near the lunch registration table; it was made of tooled brown leather and quite distinctive. I approached Joe and asked him if he had noticed any problem with security near the registration table, and he said that he had not. I then pointed to the briefcase, left unattended and near the path the Prime Minister was expected to take to enter the large hotel dining room. Joe asked me what I was worried about, which I found to be an incredible question – so incredible that I left him at once and went up to the head of the Israeli security detail just inside the dining room. I recognized him, having met him on several previous occasions. I whispered to him about the incident with the briefcase, and he went into action at once, using his radio to contact the New York Police Department staff present at the event.

A few short minutes later, several plainclothes officers arrived with a large steel drum into which the briefcase was very carefully placed. The entire operation was done so smoothly that very few of the luncheon invitees even noticed what was going on – but Joe, my boss, did. He turned very pale and moved away from his post at the registration table, in fact spending some time in the men's room while the briefcase was removed. Meanwhile, I returned to my post downstairs at one of the elevators, and said nothing to my colleague about the incident. The luncheon went quite smoothly, and I got to hear Prime Minister Rabin while I was standing up and watching the crowd. Nobody ever thanked me, and I do not know with certainty, to this day, if the briefcase had contained a bomb or merely papers. What I did know was that our security system had indeed worked flawlessly, and that all was well, at least for the moment.

There were two developments in the aftermath of that luncheon, one funny and one tragic. The amusing event involved a bet I made with ISA's New York Real Estate Director, who was also active in our Professional Personnel Group. At the next PPG meeting, I told the tale of the mysterious briefcase, and Joe's need to spend considerable time in the men's room until that briefcase was removed and the risk was over. This led to a major discussion of the lack of adequate security at the ISA national office, and ended up with a bet between the Real Estate Director and me when I stated that Yasser Arafat, the head of the Palestinian Liberation Organization, could get into our offices if he wished. For the next month's staff meeting at our New York headquarters, I wore a trench coat and an Arab-style head covering, and signed into the logbook downstairs in the ISA office building as `Y. Arafat.` I was then, without further ado, escorted upstairs to our suite of offices by a security guard for the office building. I went at once to the office of our Real Estate Director and asked him to come downstairs and look at the log book at the security desk. He saw my fake Arafat signature and, without protesting, handed me the twenty dollars we had bet. Sharing this tale led to improved security!

The tragic event was the assassination of Israeli Prime Minister Yitzhak Rabin on November 4, 1995, considerably after I had left ISA. Rabin, along with his Foreign Minister Shimon Peres and Palestinian

Liberation Organization head Yasser Arafat (in person, this time, not by proxy) had been jointly awarded the Nobel Peace Prize in 1994 for their key roles in the Oslo Peace Accords. That role, however, did not sit well with some of the militants on both sides of Israeli-Arab conflict. To encourage support in Israel for the Peace Accords, a giant peace rally was held on that November 4 date in Jerusalem. As the Prime Minister was approaching his car, a right-wing Israeli fanatic named Yigal Amir shot Rabin fatally. U.S. President, Bill Clinton, a staunch supporter of peace in the Middle East, attended the funeral, and in his brief remarks, used the Hebrew phrase, Shalom, Chaver – Peace, Brother. The cause of peace had lost a staunch ally when Rabin died. The Oslo Peace Accords, most unfortunately, never went into effect.

CHAPTER THIRTY-FIVE

◆

THE FIRST WORLD TRADE CENTER BOMBING

Because each of us becomes wrapped up in the fabric of our own individual lives, it is sometimes easy to forget that the outside world moves on around us. While I was preparing to end my tenure at the Israeli Securities Agency or ISA, a group of terrorist conspirators were planning and plotting to blow up the World Trade Center in New York City. On February 26, 1993, a car bomb was detonated below Tower One, of the gas-enhanced type similar to that used in the 1983 Beirut Marine Barracks bomb. This fifteen-hundred-pound explosive device was intended to topple Tower One, the North Tower, into Tower Two, the South Tower, in order to bring both towers down and kill thousands of innocent people. That failed to happen, but six people were killed, and 1,042 were injured, many seriously.

The bombing was planned by a group of Arab conspirators masterminded by Ramzi Yousef, whose uncle, Khalid Shaikh Mohammed, helped to finance it. (Khalid Shaikh Mohammed is considered one principal architect of the September 11, 2001 attacks.) Yousef managed to enter the United States on September 1, 1992, using a false Iraqi passport and claiming political asylum. He was allowed into the U.S. and given a hearing date on his asylum claim. Meanwhile, he set up residence in Jersey City, New Jersey, traveling around the New Jersey-New York area and contacting Sheik Omar Abdel Rahman, a blind Muslim cleric, and the other terrorist conspirators. Yousef then began assembling the bomb.

El Sayyid Nosair, one of Sheik Rahman's men, had been arrested the year before in the case of the murder of Rabbi Meir Kahane, a leader of extremist Israelis who wanted all Arabs deported from Israel. Eventually, Nosair was convicted of the charge in Federal Court. Dozens of Arabic-language bomb making manuals and documents detailing terrorist plots were found in his New Jersey apartment, including secret American military memos and 1,440 rounds of ammunition. These incidents were not put together by those investigating them, and they did not lead to the World Trade Bombing plotters in time.

After mailing letters to various New York City newspapers just before the attack, giving American support for Israel and our interference in the Middle East as reasons for the bombing, Yousef and a Jordanian, Eyad Ismoil, drove a rented yellow Ryder van into Lower Manhattan, into the public parking garage under the World Trade Center around noon. Yousef then ignited a twenty-foot fuse and took off. Twelve minutes later, at 12:17 p.m., the large, enhanced bomb exploded in the underground garage, opening a hole nearly one hundred feet wide through four concrete sublevels.

The enhanced bomb instantly cut off all power, including the emergency lighting system, and caused smoke to rise as high as the ninety-third floor of both towers. Hundreds of people were trapped in elevators when the power went off, including seventeen kindergarten children on their way down from an observation deck. It took five hours to free those trapped by the blast. But at least the World Trade Towers did not collapse; primarily the parking garage was badly damaged. Had the car been parked closer to the poured concrete foundations, the plan might have succeeded. Yousef escaped to Pakistan several hours after the bombing. There was some evidence that the United Nations Building on the East Side of midtown was the original intended target.

As a result of the loss of electricity, most of New York City's radio and television stations lost their over-the-air broadcast signal for almost a week. TV stations were only able to broadcast via cable and satellite, thanks to a microwave hookup. Telephone service for much of lower Manhattan was also disrupted. Yousef, the major bomber, wanted the smoke to remain in the tower, smothering people and killing them slowly. He later stated that he only wished he had added sodium cyanide to his bomb, to make it even more deadly. A horrid group of terrorists had perpetrated a truly horrible event.

I learned of the 1993 World Trade Center Bombing while driving from a meeting to the West Hartford ISA office. I had been listening to music on the car radio, when the program was interrupted to announce the bombing. Upon reaching my office, I turned on a small TV set there, in order to follow the ongoing coverage of that terrorist attack.

My perspective on terrorism, both then and now, differs from that of most Americans. I could not say that I was surprised by this New York bombing, not after the Marine Barracks in Lebanon had been blown up ten years earlier. I had tried my best to get our federal government to respond to the risks to those brave Marines, to no avail. Even my Congresswoman and friend, Barbara Kennelly, was unable to get the then-Secretary of Defense, Caspar Weinberger, to take any action to protect those Marines, such as the simple step of putting concrete block barricades in front of that barracks. Had that been done, the bomber's truck could not have driven right into the building, carrying a huge bomb to be set off, and costing over two hundred and forty lives.

Even before that tragic event, on my missions to Israel, I had seen the ravages of terror there: bombed-out buses, the results of suicide bombers, destroyed buildings, hostage situations, the list went on and on. Ever after the Marine Barracks bombing, I had tried to track terrorism directed against America and Americans, of which there was no shortage.

Later in 1983, the Armed Resistance Unit, a militant leftist group, bombed our Capitol in response to the U.S. invasion of Grenada. In 1984, the U.S. Embassy annex in Awkar, Lebanon, was bombed. In 1985, both TWA Flight 847 and the cruise ship Achille Lauro were hijacked. In 1986, a British discotheque bombing killed two American servicemen and injured more than fifty others. In 1987, a car bomb exploded outside the back gate of the U.S. Embassy in Rome, and mortars were fired from across the street. In 1988, a car bomb exploded in front of the USO club in Naples, killing and injuring our servicemen. Also in 1988, one of the most infamous terror events up to that time occurred: Pan Am Flight 103, heading from London to New York with 259 people aboard, was destroyed by a bomb over Lockerbie, Scotland. All aboard were killed, along with eleven people on the ground. Given all of these horrid events, it was hard for me to be very surprised by the 1993 World Trade Center bombing in New York.

I was, however, truly horrified at this latest outrage. That sense of horror stemmed not only from the event itself, but from how poorly our so-called security services handled the available advance information. As further details emerged as to the perpetrators of the bombing, I found that most of them had long records of terrorist activity. Yousef, their mastermind, had been noted coming into the United States on a fake Iraqi passport, but was still allowed to come here seeking equally-fake political asylum, being given a hearing date on the asylum claim, while he then disappeared into New Jersey. There were so many other instances of sloppy, careless, downright incompetent security work.

Something else was clear to me from the 1993 World Trade Center bombing: the terrorists would undoubtedly try again, the risks to the World Trade Towers were far from over. Those proud buildings were symbols of everything the extremists hated about the United States – they were not only the heart of our financial structure, but also the heart of America itself. The World Trade Towers were symbols of our own way of life.

It was also clear that, even if other targets were picked the next time, perhaps the Empire State Building or the Statue of Liberty, there would undoubtedly be a "next time." The terrorist forces would re-group, probably under a different name or label, and attack again. They would learn from the limited success, in their distorted view, of the 1993 attack; and weapons technology would continue to advance. By the time of the next terror attack on the United States, there would be the likelihood of much greater loss of life and much more damage. **The 9-11-2001 tragedy was predictable!**

These conclusions led me to write, phone, and email those whom I knew in Congress, to send letters to the editors of various newspapers, to produce Op-Ed pieces, and attempt to contact our alphabet-soup of safety and security agencies in Washington. Had I left my work for the State of Israel on better terms, I would have contacted their New York consulate. As it was, I sent copies of some of my commentaries to the Foreign Ministry in Jerusalem, hoping that Israelis might be able to prompt some action out of our own security services such as the Central Intelligence Agency and the National Security Agency. It was well known that Israel had the mosteffective counter-terrorism structure in the world, even if it was not always totally successful in preventing horrid attacks.

All of these efforts, though, seemed to fall on deaf ears and blind eyes. At best, there would be a polite formal letter in response; at worst, there was not even that letter. It was with a heavy heart that I finally realized that little was going to be done to ensure the safety and security of the United States from future terrorist attacks. The evil genie was out of the bottle, and nobody seemed very serious about trying to put it back once more.

CHAPTER THIRTY-SIX

◈

NORTHWARD TO VERMONT

Once again, fate, karma, or divine intervention came to me just in the nick of time. I had decided to take a weekend off and go to a classic auto show in Southern Vermont. Such cars had been a hobby of mine since my teenage days in the distant past, and I had owned some of the great ones, ranging from three Jaguars to a Studebaker Golden Hawk. This particular car show was known throughout New England as being the best one in the late fall, as the Hemmings family, publishers of the definitive guide to classic cars and based in Bennington, Vermont, was a co-sponsor of the show.

I had acquired a classic Shasta RV – a 1972 model which most would call old rather than classic – which I had named "Fasta Shasta" via a large engraved sign on its rear. So I packed up the RV, which could sleep four people if two of them did not mind being in a compartment above the driving area, and headed Northward to the Bennington show.

The car show was at the fairgrounds, and included a playground and rides for kids. After a few hours of car viewing and shopping for parts, manuals, and memorabilia, I had had enough of the show, and I headed into downtown Bennington; passing a Chinese restaurant, I remembered that I had not taken time out for lunch. On the way into the restaurant, I grabbed a real estate newspaper with advertisements for Vermont properties.

Over lunch, I was just glancing at the newspaper, when an advertisement jumped out at me, offering a "Turnkey Community Care Home in Pownal, Vermont" for sale at once. Suddenly, I felt fate take a hand once again; what a wonderful opportunity to help out elderly people and others who needed supervised living, while making an income in the process. With a turnkey operation, I would not be starting from scratch; everything that I needed would be in place. The ad even said that the former owner, a nurse, would be available to help manage the operation. From the restaurant, I called the named realtor, Fran, making an appointment to see the Pownal Community Care Home at once.

I met Fran at her office in Pownal Center, a few miles south of Bennington, and followed her to the facility. It was a large Victorian mansion just off Route 346; Pownal is the most Southwesterly town in Vermont, where that state, Massachusetts, and New York all come together. The house was in good shape, although it needed some new paint and outside cleanup. It had nine bedrooms, five baths, kitchen, living room, and dining room – and eleven residents. I was quite impressed with the place and its people, who were in their nineties but were able to carry out most of the ADLs, the activities of daily living, as needed in order to be in a community care home (otherwise, a full nursing home would be required for them, a much more costly and less home-like situation).

Driving home to Connecticut, and reviewing my options, I thought that having my own business would be a wonderful step to take, particularly if that business involved really helping those who needed assistance, such as the frail elderly. I had really liked Bennington, which has a great deal of New England charm and style. I could commute to Pownal to operate the Home, while taking the necessary nursing home manager certification course in Vermont, and return home to Connecticut on the weekends. A full nursing staff was already in place at PCCH, and they would join the former owner to get me started. The next day, I faxed an offer to buy the property to Fran, the realtor, which the seller accepted. I was becoming a Vermonter; a new phase of my life was beginning.

CHAPTER THIRTY-SEVEN

◆

WHISTLE BLOWER

I had given the top management at ISA three months to clean up their act and to meet U. S. tax laws and other requirements. Those three months ended at the end of 1993, which would also be when my term on the Board of the Professional Personnel Group, the ISA union, would end. There was only an ominous silence from my boss, Joe, and the other executives at ISA during those last three months of 1993. After that nasty call from The General in response to my ultimatum, there was no further response from my employer that fall – but I knew that this was merely the calm before the major storm. Undoubtedly, my supervisor Joe, The General, and our legal head were working urgently behind the scenes, in consultation with ISA's outside legal specialists, to find a way to deal with me as a potential tax-violations whistle-blower against the securities company.

Having had the real estate closing upon my new Vermont business in November, I was ready to leave ISA, which required one month's notice to be given. On December 1, 1993, I sent a certified letter to The General, with copies to my supervisor and the ISA legal head, announcing my resignation at the end of December, 1993. As to the reason, I gave my purchase of a business venture, with no further information provided; after that car chase incident in Hartford, I did not trust ISA and whoever else might be involved in trying to cover up their wrongful U.S. tax avoidance.

By January of 1994, I was ready to move into the basement apartment at the Pownal Community Care Home, where I would be staying until that June. Meanwhile, I would look at possible homes in Pownal or nearby Bennington, with the help of Realtor Fran. Since returning to my Connecticut home required a four-hour trip each way, I very much preferred to relocate to Bennington; Pownal was not a town where I really wanted to live, as it was rather run-down, offered few amenities, and was not much respected in Southern Vermont. I had hired an assistant manager for the Care Home so that I could come back to Connecticut most weekends, pending the permanent move to Vermont.

At the end of December, 1993, I cleaned up my affairs at ISA, said goodbye to staff (whom I had told that I was leaving at the same time I had written the ISA executives), left the keys with my assistant, and headed out the door of the West Hartford ISA office for the last time. There was a sense of real relief, of freedom, of new opportunities; I had put my Windsor, Connecticut, home on the market, and this would be the very last time I celebrated the New Year there. I was a bit sentimental over leaving, but also quite happy.

On New Year's Day 1994, after a hearty brunch, I drove to the Windsor Locks main post office, which was open around-the-clock, sending a second certified letter to the top executives at ISA. That letter reminded them that the ninety-day period I had given them to devise a plan for full tax compliance had expired – but there was more. For months, I had been investigating other ISA violations of American standards in the marketing of their securities: their failure to provide full and accurate information on their Bonds; the heavy use of excessive appeals to emotion to make sales; and particularly the sales roles of lay leaders, who were not registered representatives, as required by securities laws. I had seen my own Hartford campaign chairman sell several million dollars of our Bonds to the State of Connecticut Treasurer for political reasons, when that same chairman had no securities license allowing him to do so. In return, quid pro quo, we staged a major tribute dinner for that same State Treasurer. The Securities and Exchange Commission does not appreciate such shenanigans; selling securities without a license breaks the law.

Now, I wrote the ISA executives that, since they had failed to respond on the tax and other issues, taking no corrective action at all, each and every violation they had been committing for decades was going to be raised with the proper regulatory agencies – the IRS, SEC, NASD, and several others. While this might seem a bit harsh, it was clear to me that unless ISA cleaned up its act at once, the securities firm would just continue to exploit American friends of Israel until, sooner or later, matters would come to a head, probably resulting in a full Congressional investigation. I had seen this happen to other securities firms, those dealing in junk bonds, for example. I had witnessed the savings and loan crisis resulting from the abuses in that industry. It was only a matter of time until ISA gave the State of Israel a black eye, jeopardizing American-Israeli relations. ISA thus needed to change its ways before that happened, which the firm refused to do.

I was leaving the agency as a whistle-blower, and my whistle was blowing clearly and loudly. I had not forgotten the car chase in Hartford, when a black Ford with diplomatic plates had followed me from a gas station until I was able to shake it off my trail. At the time, I took that as a warning; and now that my information would soon be on its way to Federal and State agencies, I thought there was a likelihood that similar incidents would occur, perhaps even more serious ones. I was also worried for my family's safety. Perhaps I was being paranoid, but it is truly said that "even paranoids have enemies."

Therefore, I informed ISA in the same set of letters that I had sent sealed copies of all of my complaints to friends and associates throughout the United States and "elsewhere", with instructions to send those sealed envelopes to various news media, including the New York Times, Washington Post, and Sixty Minutes investigative journalism program, as well as my contacts in the United States Congress, should anything happen to me. I knew that these steps seemed very far-fetched – but "better safe than sorry" is my belief.

When I had first raised the possibility of filing complaints with regulatory agencies should ISA not clean up its own house, their legal director had commented that those agencies would not take any action on my complaints. She said that ISA had many powerful friends who would squash any such actions. At the time, I thought she was just puffing wind, and further, it was likely that my complaints were not the first against ISA.

In retrospect, however, it turned out that she was right, and that ISA might have the last laugh. It amazed me, as months went by with no reactions by the IRS, SEC, NASD or other government agencies to the profound illegalities I had reported at ISA, including nearly a half billion dollars of unreported and untaxed interest payments to Americans. Yes, there were form acknowledgements from the government supervisory agencies, but that was all. Following up on the complaints produced only fogging, stalling, excuses – but no actions.

I could not believe that so many Federal and State agencies could be so lax, so I asked my two members of Congress – Barbara Kennelly in Connecticut and Bernie Sanders in Vermont – to investigate. After more time elapsed, I finally got phone calls from both of their offices. What I was told, essentially, was that no agencies wanted to investigate an arm of a foreign nation, namely ISA, and particularly not a firm which was essentially part of our key ally, Israel. ISA was indeed protected in its tax and securities violations, by being part of the Israeli Finance Ministry, even though nominally it was an American corporation. Bernie Sanders' top assistant in Washington told me that the trouble which would be stirred up by investigating ISA over a 'measly few hundred million dollars' of untaxed Bond interest would be far worse than merely ignoring the issue – and much the same could be said of the many violations of our securities laws as well.

While this attitude seemed disgraceful to me, it was indeed understandable. Upon communicating with other whistle-blowers on computer websites, I found that the experience I had encountered was not uncommon; for example, the federal government had taken decades to look into charges that the tobacco companies were purposely adding nicotine to cigarettes to make them more addictive, and even worse matters. Many of the other whistle-blowers, who had been reporting waste and fraud by the government itself, experienced nothing but frustration. In many such cases, the old adage 'See no evil, Hear no evil, Speak no evil'seemed to be applied to whistle-blowers. I was far from alone.

CHAPTER THIRTY-EIGHT

◆

EMERGENCY MANAGER

In the aftermath of the 1993 World Trade Center bombing, I had vowed to do my utmost to help prevent future terrorism against the United States and its citizens around the world. That was admittedly a tall order, but I could try to do no less; rather, after failing to head off the Marine Barracks bombing tragedy ten years earlier, I believed that I had an absolute moral obligation to undertake this task. I claimed little special expertise or training, but after seeing the effects of terrorism firsthand, both in Israel and the United States, I simply had to do whatever I could. I recalled the words of the martyred U.S. Senator Robert F. Kennedy, himself the victim of terrorism, who stated: "One man can make a difference, and every man should try." It was now my turn, and time, to try.

Taking only occasional shifts at the Pownal Community Care Home I had purchased in Southern Vermont, I had spare time to learn more about terrorism and terror tactics, even its least pleasant aspects. Some of the internet resources, even back then, were amazing. One could find specific instructions to make a nuclear weapon, although some of the materials, such as plutonium or enriched uranium, might be hard to obtain. On the other hand, a "dirty bomb" consisting of radioactive materials readily available for medical uses, combined with a powerful plastic explosive, could be constructed in someone's basement or garage.

Not really being into such weapons, though, I found the websites maintained by many terrorist groups to be fascinating. Some were clearly aimed at recruiting the disaffected, often Americans who had some grievance against their nation, such as the Unabomber. Some showed a profound knowledge of human psychology, both normal and aberrant. Others provided a laundry list of possible techniques, targets, and even escape routes.

I also began to learn more about emergency management, from FEMA, the Federal Emergency Management Agency, and comparable State agencies including Vermont's. It seemed urgent to me that such disaster-prevention agencies reorient themselves to focus much more extensively on what were termed "societal disasters" such as terrorism. While natural disasters – flooding, fires, earthquakes, tornados, hurricanes and so on – would always be with us, the new direction for FEMA and similar agencies had to be the combating of terrorism and similar societal problems. The more that I learned, the more I realized that I did not know, and needed to learn. There were many sleepless nights, and others filled with nightmares, as that part of my studies on terrorism was most unpleasant.

As matters developed, I was to start out on a rather small scale, though. The big event in Bennington, Vermont, each August is the celebration of the Battle of Bennington, which appears to have been actually fought in nearby Hoosick Falls, New York. But the City of Bennington erected a sort of mini-Washington Monument to commemorate its battle, and there is a major parade as part of the annual observance.

Walking around Bennington, I noted that there were a number of paper bags along the parade route, often in the street next to the curb. While these were probably harmless, perhaps containing empty bottles of alcoholic spirits, I knew that in Israel such bags and other street debris were always a cause of concern, as on occasion they contained small explosive devices. Even if this was somebody's idea of a prank, it was still hazardous. Therefore, noting one of Bennington's finest, a police sergeant, I expressed my concern to him. The good sergeant's response was to look annoyed as he continued to drink his coffee. The brown paper bags remained along the curb, of course. That was unacceptable.

Early the following week, I submitted a series of security recommendations to the Bennington Police Department, bringing them to its headquarters in an old building. I handed them to the officer on duty and asked to see someone responsible for the parade, but was told that nobody was available at that time, so I asked for a phone call. No such phone call ever came, so I sent my recommendations to the local newspaper, the Bennington Banner, as a letter to the editor. The parade was long over by then, but there would be another one the next year.

The day my letter appeared, I got a call from the Bennington Chief of Police, who asked me who the hell I thought I was. I told him my name, in response to his rude inquiry. I also told him that I had worked security for the annual Salute to Israel parade in New York each June, which was one of my duties while working for the Israeli Securities Agency. In that capacity, I had made a number of recommendations which were adopted by the organizers of the parade, a special interagency committee in New York. The police chief then told me, "Well, this isn't New York. We don't like changes up here, and particularly not those coming from flatlanders like you." Flatlander was a real insult, I came to learn. It was obvious that my recommendations would never be judged on their merits, particularly not if they came from a "flatlander."

Thinking about the police reaction, not so much to my recommendations as to my right to make them at all, it came to me that what I really needed was an official position from which to conduct safety and security enhancements. Having noted in my research that each city and town in Vermont was supposed to have an Emergency Management Coordinator or EMC, I called the Bennington City Hall to inquire, but was told that their EMC was in place. However, I was also told that the Town of Pownal, where my Community Care Home was located, did not have an EMC, so I applied to their Board of Selectmen, the governing body, with a letter stating my background and qualifications. I was invited to the next Selectmen's meeting and appointed then and there. Technically, since I had lived in the Care Home's basement apartment and also had property in Pownal, I was entitled to residency status and therefore was eligible for the volunteer post.

Thus began an interesting period of brush clearing after storms, helping to clean up hazardous material spills, monitoring the removal of toxic wastes at the old Pownal Tannery, and warning locals when there were possible tornados or ice storms. One memorable moment was going to the American Legion, the local watering hole, to try to roust out a bunch of drunks and near-drunks after we were notified of a likely tornado, which never arrived. Another was dealing with a run-down trailer park at risk from severe flooding, where I finally had to have the power shut off to get people to go to a Red Cross shelter in a local firehouse until the flooding receded. I also got to serve on the area Local Emergency Preparedness Committee, which met monthly and included all EMCs in Bennington County; and on a Statewide ADEPT team, my acronym coined to stand for Animal Disaster Emergency Planning Team. ADEPT met in lovely Montpelier, the State capital, to devise a Vermont plan to deal with pets and farm animal issues and problems during emergencies. This was all good and meaningful volunteer work.

What was not so good, however, was the reaction to my emergency management work for the Town of Pownal. I had been a bit heavy-handed in rousting out the drunks at the American Legion, and by forcing the trailer park residents to move as floodwaters were rising. Even worse, I had made some enemies at the local firehouse by challenging their supremacy in emergency matters. While I had tried to be tactful, I found the local fire crew to be a well-intended bunch of cretins who used arrogance in place of any real expertise for firefighting. Their Women's Auxiliary mainly brought sandwiches and drinks to the firehouse for the guys. There was only one female firefighter, who was not treated with much respect.

I did not realize I had challenged the supreme authority of the Pownal volunteer firemen until I was called before the Board of Selectmen to "explain myself." When I got to the meeting, the entire leadership of the Firehouse was there, looking somewhat like a hanging jury, and sounding much the same as they recited a list of my sins. One of the worst was that, when power to the railroad crossing gates failed, I had directed traffic there for several hours so that no motorist was hit by one of the frequent freight trains. I was given an opportunity to respond to these "charges" and replied that I would not even dignify them with a response, as they were ridiculous.

What was also ridiculous was an editorial the following week, in the North Adams Transcript, a local newspaper which covered Pownal, calling me arrogant and over-eager as Emergency Management Coordinator. I replied to the editorial, which I later learned was written by the girlfriend of one of the unfriendly firemen, who was a Transcript staffer. Reading the editorial and my reply opened my eyes, and I at once agreed with it and was glad to resign the duties of Emergency Management Coordinator at the next meeting of the Board of Selectmen. Frankly, it was a real relief to be free of a nasty job.

I had the last word, literally, however. My page on EMC activities over those past two years in Pownal was already part of the Town's mandatory Annual Report, which was already printed. It was given out at the Annual Pownal Town Meeting, held at the local grade school. I got to the meeting early, grabbing a box of those Annual Reports while waiting for the entire Firehouse contingent to arrive, including the nasty Transcript reporter who had written the nasty editorial about my EMC work. As the firemen entered the school for the meeting, I handed each of them a Town Annual Report already opened to the page containing my own report. It was a real pleasure to see their startled faces, not to mention their annoyance at my report. It was the first time an EMC report had even been submitted to the Town of Pownal – and probably would be the last, as well.

◈

THE FIRE, AND FEMA

On a sunny Sunday afternoon the following April, I was having an early dinner when the phone rang; it was the Pownal fire department, which had harassed me out of being the Town Emergency Management Coordinator. But that was not why they were calling. Craig, the deputy fire chief, said, "Eugene, your Care Home is on fire. It doesn't look good." He then hung up, and I rushed out the door and into my Subaru for the short trip to the Home – which I managed to make in ten minutes flat that time.

When I arrived, smoke was pouring out of the back of the old Victorian house, and its adjacent large storage building had flames shooting out of the roof. The fire crew was trying desperately to put out the fire with hoses and extinguishers, to little apparent avail. But I have to give them full credit for trying, and for helping with evacuating our frail elderly residents. The nurse on duty had begun that evacuation as soon as she smelled smoke, not even taking time to call me; we always had monthly fire drills, as required by State law, and during those drills everyone had to be out within a few minutes. An actual fire, however, was a different matter, as then panic and mistakes occurred.

Still, by the time we arrived, all the residents were outside of the house, seated in chairs which had been removed from the living and dining rooms by the fire crew. Blankets had also been taken outside to wrap them in, and I directed further steps for their comfort and safety. The damage turned out to be sufficient to prevent their return.

Luckily, a Bennington nursing facility had room to provide temporary shelter for our residents, and I began to run a shuttle service there after calling its director. Meanwhile, the fire was extinguished, and we began to assess the situation. The fire had started in the large storage building, and I suspected that someone had been smoking in it, as smoking was not allowed in the Care Home itself. There were several possible culprits, as we had begun our Spring landscaping and gardening work that Sunday, and there were several lawn and shrub workers, all of whom smoked. (I turned that information over to the State Fire Marshal, but the fire's cause was never solved; the Fire Marshal had been termed a man who could not find his butt with both hands behind his back, which seemed fitting.)

While the damage to the Care Home itself was relatively superficial, it would take a great deal of money to meet State standards and restore it as a residential facility for frail elderly people. My insurance company claimed that they had insured it as a house, not a business, and therefore would not pay for its restoration to Vermont standards for such a facility, which are quite demanding. It seemed therefore that I was out of business, as even if I sued the insurer, that would take a long time to settle, with no guarantee of the outcome. Then it would take even longer to re-build the facility to meet State standards. I was therefore, due to the fire, now the ex-operator of Pownal Community Care.

Within a week or two, all of my former residents were placed elsewhere, either in the Bennington facility or at others nearby. I had been serving on the Board of the Vermont Health Care Association, which provided great familiarity with all the available options. We had two residents over one hundred years old, and were able to find them a location together. Insofar as possible, we kept friends together in the same new location. I did the best that I could for our people, including sometimes cutting deals to get them placed at less than the standard monthly charge if they could not afford that cost.

Now, however, being literally out of business, I needed a new professional direction. I had been teaching part time at North Adams State College, as I had previously done in Connecticut. But that would not cover my living costs, nor did I want to go through the pain and strain of job hunting in the usual fashion. I was nearing sixty, and looked it. Any potential employer was likely to think that I would be pushing up the daisies before they could recover their investment in me. Could I ever find a good job?

That was when fate, karma, or divine intervention played a hand once again. I had served as a volunteer emergency manager, not only in Pownal, but also at the county and State levels in Vermont. My motivation stemmed in part from the terrorist emergencies I had experienced, some firsthand. As Vermont volunteer, I had met a number of officials from the Federal Emergency Management Agency, Region I, in Boston, Massachusetts. On an impulse, I picked up the phone and called Kevin, with whom I had had the most contact at FEMA. Kevin was in charge of Hazard Mitigation, the division which tries to prevent disasters from happening before they occur – a daunting and fascinating task. Kevin invited me to come for some training at FEMA's Acton, Massachusetts, facility, an old Cold War bunker which could serve as a command center whenever a real disaster occurred. The session was scheduled for the following week in June of 1999.

One plus factor was that, on the way to Acton, I stopped in Lowell, Massachusetts, to visit a tavern which one of my favorite authors, Jack Kerouac, had frequented. *On The Road,* his best-known book, mentions that tavern, and I managed to find it after asking for directions. The young woman tending the bar, however, had never heard of Kerouac, or of the beatnik generation, and seemed to have little interest in the subject. Still, the bar was quiet, as it was a Sunday afternoon, and I sat on each and every barstool, since one of them had to have been Jack Kerouac's haunt. The bar lady probably thought I was crazy.

That FEMA training was fascinating, covering all aspects of emergency management, from natural disasters to societal ones such as the atrocities of terrorism. There were also sessions ranging from ethical considerations in government work to avoiding any form of sexual or other harassment. It was a very busy week, down below the ground in The Bunker, as the FEMA facility was known. I graduated from the training with high honors. On the last day, I asked Kevin, who had invited me to the session, if he knew of any hazard mitigation jobs, as that was his field and I hoped to make it my field also.

Later that year, I applied for the open hazard mitigation consultancy job at NHOEM, the New Hampshire Office of Emergency Management, based in Concord, a charming small city and the capitol of New Hampshire. The SHMO interviewed me – SHMO stands for State Hazard Mitigation Officer, and this particular SHMO, named John, shared my smile at the acronym. That shared smile started us off on the right foot, and I was offered the job on the spot. While this was a grant-funded position, which would end when its grant ran out, it was the start of a whole new career – one dealing with issues I really cared about! I could hardly wait to move to New Hampshire for new challenges.

CHAPTER FORTY

◆

THE SCOPE PROPOSAL

My new hazard mitigation consultancy called for me to begin work just after the start of 2000: the New Year and New Millennium. I had bought a Sunday Concord Monitor newspaper the previous week, when I traveled to NHOEM to complete the necessary employment paperwork. I had often thought of how nice it would be to have a house on a body of water, a river or lake, and I found only one house of that sort listed in the Monitor. It was a cottage in Hillsborough, New Hampshire, which had been converted to year-round use by a couple who were now getting ready to retire to Florida.

I met their realtor at the house, on Emerald Lake in Hillsborough. It was smaller than the home in Bennington, Vermont, now on the market, but was cozy and charming. While I was thinking about making an offer, the realtor told me confidentially that if we offered ten thousand dollars less than the asking price, it would probably be accepted. I did, and it was. I moved to Emerald Lake over the summer of 2000, with my two dogs, Tucker and Domino, with whom I had been living in an RV in Epsom, New Hampshire, commuting back to Pownal on weekends. The Hillsboro House was far more convenient.

With everything in place by the fall of 2000, I could then concentrate mainly on hazard mitigation. My immediate responsibility was to monitor nearly fifty incomplete projects all over the State of New Hampshire, driving an official vehicle and examining bridges, roads, buildings, and other infrastructure to assess the degree of their completion and the reasons for any delays. This work was absolutely fascinating; for the first time, I was using engineering skills I had studied long ago at MIT, which I was now upgrading through on-line information sources. John, the SHMO, was my mentor, and while he was a hard taskmaster, his computer skills were outstanding. Thus, I was learning by doing.

There was a downside to my position, however. It was funded out of FEMA money given to New Hampshire as a result of Hurricane Floyd, money that was running out. I would be paid from those funds for a little over a year, and then they would be gone. It was up to me to secure completion of all outstanding hazard mitigation projects by then. So, I was working myself out of a job.

As the end of the FEMA funding began to approach, I devised a plan to continue my hazard mitigation work. I produced the SCOPE Program proposal.* SCOPE stands for Safer Communities through Organized Preventive Effort, and was the logical extension of my hazard mitigation work. Through a series of systematic steps, any community, town, or city anywhere could assess its specific needs in various areas of hazard mitigation – exactly what it needed to do to reduce or even prevent disasters from occurring. It is truly said that **an ounce of prevention is worth a pound of cure**, and I had designed the blueprint for that vital ounce. I then shared SCOPE with John, my boss and mentor, but his reaction surprised me. I did not know John as well as I had thought.

John blew his cool, telling me that I had some nerve to be designing hazard mitigation programs on "his time." I told him, truthfully, that I had done the work on SCOPE at home, in my own time, but that did not seem to matter. He began to rant and rave, telling me that I was insubordinate and had betrayed him. I had taken as much as I could, and by then the shock had worn off, so I just said, "You know, John, you really need professional help – and that type of help is not my field!" [*Appendix I contains SCOPE]

Not totally deterred by John's negative reaction to SCOPE, I next presented it to Ed, the deputy director of the New Hampshire Office of Emergency Management, who seemed quite impressed and said he would present SCOPE to Woody, head of NHOEM.

Woody himself called me into his office, which I thought to be a very good sign for me and for SCOPE. I was ready to try its approach out on a few sample communities, with Woody's blessing. But, instead, Woody told me, "Eugene, you have devised a brilliant proposal. SCOPE has even been reviewed by the Governor's staff. It might well be a pilot project for the nation, which would be a real feather in our cap at NHOEM – but there is no money or budget for it; the FEMA Hurricane Floyd funds for your work are nearly gone, as you know. Still, SCOPE is such a great concept that we are going to have an intern work further on it. That way, the further work won't cost us very much."

I confess to being stunned by what sounded like a totally asinine and unfeasible way to handle the SCOPE proposal. After a moment, I said to Woody, "You know, Woody, I attended the University of Pennsylvania, which was founded by Benjamin Franklin, also one of America's founders. I wonder what would have happened to this nation if old Ben had said that a Declaration of Independence from England was a good idea, and maybe our founders could get some scribe to write it up. This is my project. I am best equipped to implement it. If NHOEM thinks differently, that is not only NHOEM's loss, but a loss to the field of hazard mitigation as well." With that said, I stormed out of Woody's office.

When I arrived home in Hillsborough that evening, I began to think of another way to promote SCOPE: **why not send SCOPE to my contacts at FEMA?** It was worth a try. That was just what I did, the next day, along with a cover letter explaining that NHOEM endorsed the SCOPE concept but claimed there were no funds for it. A few days later, not having heard back from FEMA, I called Kevin, the hazard mitigation head in Boston, who confirmed that he had received the proposal and had sent it on to FEMA in Washington. I never heard anything further; that might have been SCOPE's sad ending.

Since my project monitoring work was winding down at NHOEM, and since Woody had a positive attitude towards SCOPE (but no funds for it), I decided to try it out on a pilot basis in a few of my communities: those which had now completed their hazard mitigation projects and could devote time to the broader safety and security picture. In three trial runs, I worked with various community leaders to first assess the needs of each community in various areas of hazard mitigation – police and fire protection, public works, infrastructure, emergency preparedness, and so on. Particular importance was given to first responders, who are often left out of the loop when it comes to hazard mitigation input. The various responses were then tabulated, prioritized, and made into a communitywide questionnaire which was submitted to their next Town Meetings. The questionnaires which were returned (not as many as might have been wished) were then tabulated and analyzed, and a set of recommendations developed, in order of importance. Had SCOPE actually been in place, and not just a trial run, it would have been up to each community's mayor or governing body to then implement those recommendations. **Yes, there is still hope for SCOPE!** (see Appendix I)

CHAPTER FORTY-ONE

◆

SEPTEMBER 11, 2001

Meanwhile, my assigned hazard mitigation projects were winding down as I continued to work myself out of a job – but then, my funding was winding down, too. This led to my taking my tasks at NHOEM a bit more lightly, as I did not want to finish them while funds were still available. That was one reason I had time for a few SCOPE pilot projects, which I mostly carried out on my own time anyway. But I tended now to spend more time in my office cubby, putting the finishing touches on reports and other paperwork, rather than traveling around New Hampshire. I still had a dozen open hazard mitigation projects; when they were done, so was I.

Just before nine a.m. on September 11, 2001, I heard a commotion out in the hall. We had a number of jokers at New Hampshire Emergency Management; Gregg, a former Coast Guard officer whose office was across from my office, often joined me in pranks such as a song we composed called The Hazard Mitigation March, a song which used every word we could think of that rhymed with "mitigation" – including a couple of obscene ones. So, I thought it was a prank when Gregg burst into my office along with Lee, our planning head, and screamed, "A plane has just hit one of the World Trade Towers. Smoke is pouring out, and it looks like a major disaster." When I realized they were serious, my immediate reaction was, "It sounds like the evil work of Al Qaeda terrorists." We rushed downstairs to the basement NHOEM Operations

Room, equipped with several television sets and all sorts of hi-tech communication equipment.

A crowd was already gathered, sitting at the many desks normally designated for various emergency management specialties – several police and fire units, other first responders, and of course our own staff. We stared in horror at the photos of the first tower to be hit, and a few minutes later our horror became even worse as we saw a second plane hit the other tower. All of us know the rest of that day's nightmare, and its aftermath, culminating in the so-called "War on Terror" with its ineffective leadership.

Several staffers who had heard my comment about Al Qaeda on that morning of infamy asked me who or what Al Qaeda was, and I replied that it was perhaps the worst thing in the world. I had read about that premier terrorist group while studying the subject after the first World Trade Towers bombing in 1993. Al Qaeda was not then the recognized name of arch-terrorist Osama Bin Laden's group, but I had kept up with my terrorist research ever since that 1993 bombing. I knew that it would happen again, and actually had expected another major incident before 2001 – but during the interim period, the various terrorist groups seemed to prefer to hit American and other targets abroad.

I had suspected that the forces of terror were just biding their time, while sleeper cells were established in the United States and elsewhere. The handwriting was clear on what was left of the walls of the U.S. embassies in Kenya and Tanzania, which suffered major bombings in 1998. That handwriting became even clearer when the ship USS Cole was attacked in 2000 while in port, killing seventeen sailors and injuring another thirty-nine. And those were only the major incidents; less-dramatic terrorist acts often received little news coverage, as Americans were, sadly, coming to take them in stride. **It is indeed amazing what people can get used to, and how horrors can even become banal.** But none of these attacks had become banal or routine to me; I continued to monitor all of them, writing articles and Op-Ed pieces, contacting members of Congress, as well as the FBI, CIA, National Security Council, and the other security agencies "protecting us".(?)

CHAPTER FORTY-TWO

◈

THE CENTURION PROGRAM

There is a story about two men walking down the street of Anytown, USA. One man says to the other, "Don't you agree that the two worst things in the world are ignorance and apathy?" The second man replies, "I don't know and I don't care." No, it's not really funny. I discovered, in the wake of those abominable September 11, 2001 attacks, that I was that story's **first man**, and those alphabet-soup Federal agencies charged with our safety had far too many of those **second men**. They did not seem to know or to care. **They had not learned much from terrorism of the recent past; but, as philosopher George Santayana truly noted, they were likely to be condemned to repeat blunders.**

My watchwords for many decades had been: **Never Give In and Never Give Up.** Now, I added a third pair of watchwords which came out of the Nazi Holocaust: **Never Again.** I began to think of that set of watchwords as **"my three Nevers"**.

Watchwords are all very well, but the mitigation of the hazards of terrorism and terror attacks would take much more than words. So, I began to think about what "deeds" could supplement those "words." While my SCOPE proposal would be a step in the right direction, it would not be sufficient. SCOPE visualized a needs assessment for every town, city, and community in America, and could certainly begin with those most at risk. Those assessments could concentrate first on societal risks and threats of terrorism and terror tactics. In New Hampshire, for instance, the city of Portsmouth was deluged with sealed containers brought in on freighter ships, and nobody really knew what was in those containers. It would be amazingly easy for terrorists to bring in explosive material, even a "dirty bomb" – one with radioactive components – in that fashion, and detonate it at will. That type of scary scenario could be mitigated by SCOPE, but human intervention is absolutely essential to prevent the implementation of many threats.

Each time I had traveled on a Mission to Israel, I had been very impressed with that nation's valiant Home Guard, a cadre of trained, dedicated, and committed Israelis who watched each neighborhood on a very-local basis. They knew just what to watch for, and what steps to take when a problem occurred, or even a potential problem. They would never have allowed the brown bags I had seen along the parade route for Bennington Battle Day to just be left lying there, the way the Bennington Police Department and Vermont State Police had done. **Some version of that Home Guard approach was vital to American security – it was essential to design and implement an American Home Guard program.**

Thus, my Centurion Program was born.** *Why not encourage one in one hundred Americans, over three million in total, to volunteer for the responsibilities of "watching the watchers" – and of knowing whom to contact when something was out of line, some situation did not add up, we were at risk. Israel did this; why not the U.S.?* It took a month to design the specific Centurion Program, which I had first drafted up in 1998 in an article written for the North Adams Transcript, a newspaper for which I wrote a regular column. That article, titled "We Are Not Defenseless Against Terrorism", was picked up and reprinted by other newspapers in New England, and I had sent copies to "the usual suspects" as the saying goes: all open and hidden Federal security agencies.

As usual, those agencies had sat on the article and done nothing – just as (we learned after September 11, 2001) those same agencies, the CIA, FBI, National Security Council, and others, had ignored documents in their possession outlining the plot to blow up our World Trade Towers, Pentagon, and another target in Washington, possibly the Capitol.

We would never know the identity of that other target with certainty, as the brave people on the fourth hijacked flight forced it down in a Pennsylvania field. Tragically, however, the FBI had ignored specific intelligence about students in flight schools who had no interest in learning how to land a jetliner, just how to fly it once it was in the air. That should have been the reddest of red flags, but instead the FBI sat on the information.

The Centurion Program might well have avoided, prevented, or at least mitigated the horror of September 11, 2001. I had developed some specific scenarios of how that avoidance, prevention, or mitigation would have happened through the intervention of a trained cadre of Centurions, a Home Guard who knew what to watch for, and how to handle it. I developed pilot scenarios of how dangerous containers could be tracked in Portsmouth, and how potential destruction of dams in New Hampshire was preventable.

I sent the Centurion Program through channels to FEMA, the Pentagon, the Joint Chiefs of Staff, each of the military services, and the Army War College, which had advertised for proposals. I sent Centurion to the newly-created Department of Homeland Security, whose head instead came up with a color-coded threat level system as the cure for our risk. He was replaced but his replacement had some personal issues causing him, in turn, to be forced out also. I was reminded of the old silent movies about the Keystone Cops, a group of bunglers who "could not find their butts with both hands behind their backs." I imagined Osama Bin Laden and Al Qaeda laughing at our efforts.

You know the rest, of course. None of the agencies listened, nobody took real steps to make America safer and more secure from terrorism and terrorists. The best I received was polite thanks for submitting Centurion to them, along with an unfulfilled promise to get back to me. The worst I received was for Centurion to either be totally ignored, or to be told that there was no money for such a program.

But there was plenty of money for "goodies" parading under the rubric of Homeland Security. One of the last meetings which I attended at New Hampshire Emergency Management, just before my hazard mitigation grant ran out, featured Woody, our head, telling us that New Hampshire would receive several million dollars of Homeland Security funds, so we should put in a "wish list" of items we had wanted but could not afford. Then there was an open discussion of some of those items, ranging from the unnecessary to the bizarre. I sat there in disgust, thinking of nearly three thousand people, not only from America but other nations as well, whose deaths on September 11, 2001 might have been prevented by a real homeland security effort, including Centurion. Instead, NHOEM staff fantasized about gadgets, gimmicks, and general silliness, just to use up the cornucopia of funds. I made a few mild comments to that effect, and received mostly frowns for my attempt to focus the staff on New Hampshire's real security needs.

And that is where matters stand, at least for now – and, tragically, for the foreseeable future. America, and particularly emergency and counter-terrorism agencies charged with maintaining our safety and security, have been lucky ever since September 11, 2001; nor are all of their efforts totally wasted. **But where is the sense of vision, the overall coordination, the vital innovative approaches to the scourge of terrorism?** There is no SCOPE and no Centurion Program. Nobody is effectively "watching the watchers", and nobody, no agency, is really working effectively on turning the tides of terrorism. America cannot rely on national security continuing much longer; action is vital now!

** In the Roman Army, a Centurion was in charge of 100 soldiers. See Appendix II.

CHAPTER FORTY-THREE

◆

BIRGIT

{Anyone who has made it this far through *Never Give In; Never Give Up* has probably wondered at the lack of its author's "personal life" being included in these pages. That omission is intentional, as the purpose of this book is to cover both history and current issues, rather than private matters. However, vital personal developments occurred in 2000 which changed my life for the better, and forever, and they are therefore recounted now.}

While working in hazard mitigation for the New Hampshire Office of Emergency Management, I had been commuting between Concord and my then-home in Pownal, Vermont on weekends. In Pownal, I was living in the former Pownal Community Care Home, having sold my house there since I needed the funds more than the house. My two dogs, Tucker and Domino, accompanied me on trips between my Southwind RV parked at a campground in Epsom, NH, and the now-closed Community Care Home in Vermont.

Just to further complicate matters, I had also returned to part-time economics teaching, via Plymouth State College in Plymouth, New Hampshire, which became a university while I was there. Since my hazard mitigation work was less than full-time, and I had missed teaching for several years, the Plymouth opening was a natural for me, and I had even helped to design the school's new First Year Seminar on critical thinking.

Student advising was among my duties for Plymouth, and I began to email with a student financial aid advisor at the flagship University of New Hampshire in Durham. Soon, our emails became a bit personal, and I discovered that she was from Gotland, Sweden and had moved to America many years previously; first to New York City, then to Georgia, and now to New Hampshire. Birgit had just gone through a difficult divorce, as I had too.

Thus, we struck up an on-line friendship, and decided to meet for lunch in Portsmouth, New Hampshire, on June 10, 2001. I had kept that day open for an interview for a Town Manager job in a community on the way to Portsmouth, so I arrived at the Stockpot Restaurant for our meeting in a brown suit with white summer shoes. Birgit arrived looking much better than I did, and I was immediately impressed with her intelligence, charm, wit, and even her slight Swedish accent. I fell head over heels in love, at once.

Birgit and I began to see each other, mainly in Dover, New Hampshire, when she moved there. We were thoroughly bonded by then, spending most evenings together, often with Domino's Pizza for dinner and a Blockbuster video for entertainment. We became quite close, and were married at Dover City Hall on December 20, 2002. We began to share an apartment in Farmington, New Hampshire, so that she could commute to her job at the University of New Hampshire, while I commuted to Plymouth to teach college courses.

After the end of my hazard mitigation work at New Hampshire Emergency Management, I consulted with Birgit and decided to take on the new role of Animal Control Officer for the Farmington Police Department. While I had always loved companion animals (aka, pets), I needed training to take on the duties of an ACO, which was provided to me. With some of my duties, such as conducting an annual Rabies Vaccination Clinic, Birgit joined in the work; then, I was made deputy code enforcer and public health officer. It was a busy time, including our work for Senator John Kerry's presidential candidacy that year.

CHAPTER FORTY-FOUR

◆

HEADING SOUTH TO GEORGIA

We spent many good years in New Hampshire, even after Birgit retired from her position at the University of New Hampshire in 2006. We celebrated her retirement with a monumental touring trip of well over 12,000 miles, in her Toyota Corolla, through the entire United States and much of Canada, visiting with family and friends along the way. But, the winds of change were still blowing, as much of our immediate family had moved south to the State of Georgia, and so we decided to follow their example late in 2007.

By then, we were already spending a good part of each year in Birgit's homeland of Gotland, Sweden, a large island in the Baltic Sea which I had first visited after meeting Birgit. We had purchased a house in rural Gotland by the time of her retirement, and from that base we reached out to her son Anders and daughter-in-law Debi in Georgia, asking their help designing a house for us, near them and her daughter Amy in Atlanta.

Late in December 2007 we headed south to Georgia, but did not quite make it in our original Chevy Blazer (which had also been my animal control vehicle). Heading down the New Jersey Turnpike, not far from Philadelphia, the newly-renovated brakes went out on the Blazer, causing me to rear-end another car, after losing all brake fluid. Luckily, the car was only traveling thirty miles an hour because of a traffic jam on the Pike – so there were no injuries, and not even a traffic citation for anyone. But our car was a total loss.

We got really lucky at that point; Birgit and I found a nearby car dealer who had one vehicle which would hold everything we were moving in the Blazer: a 2006 Jeep Grand Cherokee which had been reduced in price because of being a "thirty-day unit," meaning it had been on the car dealer's lot for over a month. We bought it on the spot, moved everything from the towed Blazer to the Jeep, and were on our way the very next day.

Arriving at our new home in Dahlonega, Georgia – a small college town in the foothills of the Smoky Mountains – we began a new life in the Peachtree State. After teaching one semester at the local military university, I switched to a liberal arts college in nearby Gainesville, Georgia, where I taught a wide variety of courses for the next thirteen years (teaching only on-line after moving from Georgia). Birgit enjoyed her own retirement with a wide variety of activities, including the Garden Club and making many great friendships. We toured the Southland, from the Georgia and Carolina coasts down to Key West, Florida, where we traveled with our best friends from Gotland, Sweden.

Truth to tell, though, I never totally took to the South or Georgia. My own outlets included helping found the Stonepile Writers Group at that nearby military university, and two terms chairing the local Lumpkin County Democrats. But the South made me a bit restless after a few years, or perhaps it was those accumulating years having that effect. We began to spend more and more time at our home in rural Gotland, Sweden, where I actually felt more athome than in the American South.

Ironically, my last name is a Swedish name, even though I have no Swedish ancestry myself. That name was changed when my paternal grandfather came through Ellis Island in New York as an immigrant from his native Austria. So, perhaps it was fated that I would end up in Sweden, but it took Birgit to actually make it happen. First, though, we made one more move within the U.S.A. – from North Georgia to Southern California.

CHAPTER FORTY-FIVE

◆

HEADING WEST TO SOCAL

After returning from Sweden in the fall of 2016, Birgit and I flew to Los Angeles to see her daughter Amy, who had moved from Atlanta to Southern California a few years earlier to pursue her career as a freelance television producer. Amy showed us an unusual photo; it was a sonogram showing that she was pregnant, an event for which we had fervently hoped. Birgit had promised Amy that she would move nearby to help with the new family member, so that we could get to know the baby while Amy continued her satisfying career. So, we put our Georgia home on the market and moved once more!

Upon arriving in Southern California, we first lived in a house right across Gower Street from Amy, as its owners were temporarily in England. When they returned to L.A., we relocated down the street in The Nest, a house with a great view of the area.

The following year, we moved to Temple Hill Drive, a ten-minute walk to Amy's house. Her son, Bennett, was born on April 23 of that year, and we were overjoyed!

The following year, we all moved together to Long Beach, California. To get a feel for living on the SoCal coast, we first lived in a condo at Marina Pacifica, where we all could walk to a large shopping center by crossing a bridge over an inlet of the Pacific. Bennett was walking by that time, and we often escorted him across that bridge, or to a natural pond at Marina Pacifica featuring birds, ducks, and water turtles as attractions.

Then, after learning that we loved Long Beach, we all moved together to a vacant house in the Belmont Shore area, a couple of miles from Marina Pacifica. We could walk from there to several beaches, on the Pacific or the nearby inlet at Naples, California, or to a wide range of eateries and boutiques along East Second Street in Belmont Shore.

We really enjoyed living with Amy and Bennett, watching him grow and taking him to various programs at local libraries in Long Beach and Seal Beach. Bennett was even introduced to music through a preschool music class taught by a skilled woman who had come to SoCal from Poland many years before. All of us took to the laid-back SoCal lifestyle, although the high levels of rents and prices there were not so enjoyable. I had continued to teach economics courses for Brenau University in Georgia – now, on- line.

Shortly after moving to Belmont Shore, the COVID-19 crisis hit the world, including Southern California, and for the next two years, we were locked into living at home. We could not go anywhere without being masked and distanced, as hundreds of thousands of Americans contracted the new disease, and tens of thousands died from it. This type of tragedy had never been envisioned by any of us, and we shared the wait for vaccines to be developed against COVID-19. Birgit and I were among the first to get vaccinated in Long Beach, and we were able to make plans to return to Gotland, Sweden once more. Those plans came to fruition early in 2021, and we were finally able to live in our new apartment in Visby, Gotland's world heritage city with its ancient wall. **We were home!**

CHAPTER FORTY-SIX

◆

VISBY, GOTLAND – AND LONG BEACH, CALIFORNIA

Birgit and I had been coming regularly to Gotland, and living there for extended periods, for nearly twenty years by then. Birgit was born in Klintehamn, a small coastal city; her family had moved to the capital of Gotland, Visby, when she was quite young. She grew up in Visby, traveled to the Swedish capital of Stockholm as a young adult, and then moved to New York City in the United States, where her sister Trudi had previously re-located. Birgit took to America, becoming a U.S. citizen (while retaining Swedish citizenship) in 2016.

Our first two houses on Gotland were in rural areas of the large island in the Baltic Sea. We acquired that first house on our way off the island, literally heading for the ferry to the Swedish mainland and then to Arlanda Airport so we could fly back to the U.S.A. We had a bit of extra time before the ferry left Visby, so we looked at a realtor's listings and found a very affordable home in Hejde, lacking some amenities: what would perhaps be termed a Starter Home in America. We bought that house on the spot and lived in it for some years; Hejde is not far from Klintehamn, on the Baltic and Birgit's birthplace. In 2010, we relocated to a larger villa in Stånga, near the South Gotland regional capital of Hemse. We lived in our Stånga Villa for many years, making many great friends there, and touring much of Europe from that base,

171

including Greece, Italy, France, and Norway. That same year, I received Permanent Swedish Residency from Migrationsverket agency,

We had decided to relocate to Gotland's capital, Visby, a walled medieval city, in 2019. Visby is considerably more convenient for shopping and amenities than is rural Gotland. We found an excellent apartment which even had an elevator, rather a rarity on Gotland. After moving into our new Gotland location in the fall of 2019, we returned to So Call for what was intended to be a relatively short visit with Amy, Bennett, and other family there.

Then the COVID-19 pandemic hit, and we could not travel for nearly two years. We were essentially stranded in Long Beach, California, together with Amy and Bennett. While all of us living together had its advantages, not being able to travel had many costs, both direct (excessive California rents and prices) and indirect (really missing Gotland!)

It is truly said (perhaps first by the poet Robert Burns) that the best-laid plans of mice and men often go awry. My plan for Spring 2020 had been to serve once again as a U.S. Decennial Census Official, as I had in the two previous Constitutionally-mandated counts of all those living within the borders of the United States. In 2000 I had been census staff in Vermont and the Pioneer Valley of Massachusetts, and in 2010 I was based in North Georgia. So, serving in Long Beach, California in 2020 was a natural for me – until the misguided census office there, supported by cretins on Los Angeles Census 2020 staff, demanded that us 2020 census takers violate all local, regional, and State quarantines by interviewing non-respondents unmasked, undistanced, and unsafe from COVID-19 risks. Rather than put my family at risk of a serious disease, I fought these unsafe Census 2020 policies – first at the local level, then beyond, and eventually in Washington via efforts of members of Congress. The outcome is still uncertain, but the effort is surely worthwhile!

CHAPTER FORTY-SEVEN

◆

RETURN TO SWEDEN, AND WORLD AFFAIRS

In the Spring of 2021, Birgit and I were once more able to return to Sweden, after nearly two years away, due to the COVID-19 pandemic. We had gotten all needed vaccinations and pre-flight tests, allowing us to board a Scandinavian Airlines plane in Los Angeles and be in Gotland, Sweden, the following day, where time is nine hours later than Pacific Time. Our new apartment in Visby, Gotland's capital city, had been vacant for that entire time, so we were very excited to return there once more, and to see relatives and friends once again. As born travelers, we really resented being closed-in.

Early the following year, after many years of thought and much discussion, I took the big step of applying for Swedish citizenship, in order to become an American Swede with dual citizenship in both nations. My only hesitation was whether or not I was worthy of such a great honor, as my Swedish is nothing to brag about, and becoming part of such a great and historic nation was a big step.

While working for the State of Israel, I had been offered Israeli citizenship – and had settled for being made an honorary member of their Air Force Command on Masada. My reasons for resisting Israeli citizenship had to do with my strong dissent over some Israeli policies, which I believed then, and still believe today, are doing a grave disservice to the cause of peace in the Middle East. There is fault on both sides of the long-standing Arab-Israeli conflict, and I am still awaiting the fulfillment of the Biblical promise that Israel shall become "a light unto the nations." Matters are not moving much in that direction!

In the case of Sweden however, and with Birgit's enthusiastic backing, I came to realize that becoming Svensk would also make me a citizen of the European Union as well; I had been a supporter of the EU ever since it emerged from the ashes of World War II, seeing the combination of the EU and the North Atlantic Treaty Organization as the best defense of Western Europe against several rapacious nations to the East, including first the Soviet Union and then its successor, Russia, as well as militant and strong China.

Just before Sweden's National Day, also called Flag Day, June 6, 2022, I was granted full Swedish citizenship – it was one of the proudest days of my life, and since then I have been working diligently to offer some service back to my new nation which would justify its faith in me. I volunteered with Uppsala University, for whose Campus Gotland branch I had served on an International Scholars Committee some years previously.

CHAPTER FORTY-EIGHT

◈

UKRAINE AND NATO

Perhaps the world should have learned by now that the only constancy is change, as Buddha taught several thousand years ago. Early in 2022, the world reeled as Russia placed several hundred thousand military troops, and immense amounts of weapons and equipment, on the borders of the fully-independent nation of Ukraine to the West. For some weeks, we all were told that those troops and equipment were merely part of some "military exercise" being carried out by Russian President, Vladimir Putin. It was only when the borders of Ukraine were crossed in February, 2022 that the truth was more than confirmed: a deranged Russian dictator was invading the democratic neighbor, Ukraine!

A few days after that invasion began, I wrote and submitted worldwide an Op-Ed (here reprinted as Appendix III) which fully justified the declaration of the Russian President as a War Criminal, to be condemned as such and immediately prosecuted in world criminal courts, as were the ilk of Slobodan Milosevich as a result of the Balkan War in the 1990s, and many others as well. As the horrid destruction of a totally-blameless and proud nation continued and worsened, I wrote further articles, such as Appendix IV of this book, **Turning the Tide of Terror in Ukraine,** in an attempt to secure effectively both condemnation of what was occurring, and prevention of any such future invasions. The impetus for such articles is the apparent ineffectiveness of world bodies such as the United Nations which have tragically failed the challenge of Ukraine.

It is, indeed, hard to believe that, in our so-called Civilized Twenty-First Century World, the leader of a major world power can succeed in destroying a large neighboring nation at that leader's misguided will, while the rest of the world is willing and/or able to take no effective preventive action. While many other nations have sent major military, economic, and humanitarian aid to Ukraine, those same nations and many international bodies have failed miserably at putting an end to that nation's destruction. Perhaps what is needed is the removal of the source of the Ukraine Invasion itself – and, beyond that, the implementation of real measures to prevent any and all future "Ukraines." Of course, such steps had been taken in the recent past, while the world continued to "slip and slide" into both new major conflicts and the endless escalation of old ones. I began to believe that it was the human race itself which is fatally flawed, and that **we could not be both human and humane at the same time** – a heartrending view, which I hoped was untrue.

CHAPTER FORTY-NINE

◆

EXPATRIATION?

As the November 2022 American mid-term elections approached, and having returned to California to be with our immediate family there as well as to vote in the vital elections, I felt a growing sense of futility, a deep malaise as all the prognosticators and their ilk made clear that the United States of America was soon to be inundated in a "Red Wave" of anti-democratic (and, of course, anti-Democrats) election results which would wear away, or even wash away, the social progress of the past eighty years. Social Security and Medicare, once bedrock commitments upon which our very future would depend, would be gutted by the incoming Congress, as had already occurred in other vital areas. The endless lies and distortions about "fake elections" would take hold in a tired nation, while the last vestiges of common decency and simple humanity would become obsolete.

In the face of all of these soon-to-be-realized negative projections, I grappled with a wide range of choices and options, deciding tentatively to become an expatriate from America. This was no longer my native land; my original nation had abandoned sanity in favor of madness, with self-contradictory conspiracy theories replacing common sense and caring.

While the mishandled insurrection at the U.S. Capitol on January 6, 2021 was the most visible sign of America's decline from national sanity, the intervening period had resulted mainly in reducing the voting rights of our citizens, and even the rights of women to have control of their own bodies. *It was high time to consider options to living in America.*

Based on this decision, I decided to study the lives and backgrounds of noted American authors and artists who became known as The Lost Generation after leaving for Paris one hundred years ago. Such figures as Ernest Hemingway, T. S. Eliot, Gertrude Stein, F. Scott Fitzgerald, Ezra Pound, and others, found the freedom and experimentation which Paris encouraged and enhanced in the 1920s to be a magnet for such expatriates. Perhaps it was time for this American Swede to take a similar step now, by leaving the U.S.A. and living only on the Island of Gotland, Sweden, my new homeland. Sweden itself had also taken a "turn to the right" in its recent national and local elections, but that re-direction was a rational choice based on changed world conditions, rather than deranged madness.

My study of The Lost Generation began with Paul Brody's book titled *The Expatriates*, and continued on the Internet; what I learned was that expatriation was mainly a phase, as most of these displaced American authors and artists returned home to the U.S.A. after the Great Depression afflicted most of the Western World. While the horrors of World War I motivated their expatriation, along with America's rejection of the League of Nations intended to prevent any such future wars, combined with unworkable Prohibition of all alcoholic beverages such as wine and liquor, the severe economic disaster of the Great Depression inevitably changed the freedom and nature of avant-garde Paris in ways unattractive and unacceptable to The Lost Generation; expatriation became unattractive.

Meanwhile, while reviewing my options in the event of one more United States' electoral disaster, it turned out that the pundits were wrong: the predicted Red Wave did not sweep the nation, and Americans came partway to their senses. Perhaps America's *era of error* is ending, and the nation will once more be a beacon of progress and hope for the world. We hope to continue to live on two continents; expatriation is out – for now, at least.

CHAPTER FIFTY

◆

THE HOPEFUL FUTURE

Yes, there is hope! We must hope that the **Best of the West** are smarter, more just, and more competent than our opponents. We must hope to have the courage to change what needs to be changed, and to do so now. We need not take the stance of that apocryphal elected leader who was asked by a TV interviewer, "Don't you think the worst two things in the world are ignorance and apathy?" The official is said to have replied, "I don't know and I don't care!" *It is up to all humanity to both know and care about our world.*

Indeed, it is an absolute moral imperative to both know and care – and often, **when we cannot change the world around us, we can still change ourselves; that is the path of wisdom.** According to the very-ancient Greek myth: *After Pandora's Box was opened, unleashing all of the World's ills and evils, that Box still contained* **Hope. *We must hope.***

We must never give in. We must never give up. And, we must never forget. Shalom!

Eugene Elander, Valley Village, California, USA & Visby, Gotland, Sweden Nov. 2022

AFTERWORDS FOR
"NEVER GIVE IN, NEVER GIVE UP":

◈

AMERICA, WHERE HAVE YOU GONE?

"My country, tis of thee;
Sweet land of liberty":
Where have you gone?

Once "Land of Pilgrims' pride,
Land where our fathers died";
This fear I cannot hide:
Where have you gone?

Home of so many dreams,
Fertile fields, gracious streams:
Where have you gone?

Tall mountains, capped with snow;
Peaceful folk, down below:
Where have you gone?

Farmers tilling their fields,
Bringing forth healthy yields:
Where have you gone?

Proud workers, strong and smart,
Toiling with mind and heart:
Where have you gone?

Noble nation, brave and free,
Cradle of true democracy:
WHERE HAVE YOU GONE?

by Eugene F. Elander
Yom Kippur – October 4, 2022

According to the website Greek Myths and Greek Mythology: (*slightly edited*)

The Original Myth Of Pandora's Box:

The **myth of Pandora's box** is considered one of the most descriptive myths of human behavior in Greek mythology. Ancient Greeks used this myth not only to instruct themselves about the weaknesses of humans, but also to explain several misfortunes of the human race.

Pandora was, according to the myth, the first woman on Earth. She was created by gods; each one of them gave her a gift, thus, her name in Greek means "the one who bears all gifts". Pandora was created as a punishment to mankind; Zeus wanted to punish people because Prometheus stole fire to give it to them. Her gifts were beautifully evil, according to Hesiod. Hephaestus created her from clay, shaping her perfectly, Aphrodite gave her femininity and Athena taught her crafts. Hermes was ordered by Zeus to teach her to be deceitful, stubborn and curious.

Pandora was given a box or a jar, called "pithos" in Greek. The gods told her that the box contained special gifts from them – but she was not allowed to open the box, ever. Then Hermes took her to Epimetheus, brother of Prometheus, to be his wife. Prometheus had advised Epimetheus not to accept anything from the gods, but he saw Pandora and was astonished by her beauty; thus, he accepted her immediately.

Pandora was trying to tame her curiosity, but in the end she could not; she opened the box and all the illnesses and hardships that the gods had hidden in the box started coming out. Pandora was scared as she saw all of the evils coming out and tried to close the box as fast as possible, thus closing Hope inside. According to Hesiod, Hope indeed stayed inside because that was Zeus' will; he wanted to let people suffer in order to understand that they should not disobey their gods. Pandora was the right person to do it, because she was curious, but not malicious. **Hope remains our destiny.**

Humanity and the Multiverse

Turning our tides would seem to be an awesome task;
Then, **Why Bother To Try?,** many will ask:
Perhaps man's inhumanity to fellow man,
Is merely part of some great Master Plan;
Perhaps inhumanity has indeed come to stay,
And terror tactics will truly rule our day –
As our universe is ruled by entropy:
Everything just keeps on getting worse, you see.

Yet – entropy itself no longer rules
The physics that once I learned in schools;
For it seems that, in our complex multiverse,
Matters, indeed, need not keep getting worse;
Even should this universe fulfill our worst fears,
Its end will not come for many billion years;
In fact, our universe itself may rise again,
So, why not keep an open mind until then?

Much nearer in time, we find glimmers of hope,
For humanity has not yet reached full Scope;
Earth's been around for some four billion years,
Meaning: our small share of time just disappears;
We're the "new kids on the block" with a lot to learn –
But there are signs of progress which we can discern;
Let's not be quite so quick to put humanity down:
For the moment, we are *the only game in town.*

APPENDIX I
ON THE SCOPE PROPOSAL:

◈

SCOPE (Safer Communities through Organized Preventive Effort) was developed by Eugene F. Elander while serving as hazard mitigation consultant to the New Hampshire Office of Emergency Management, based in Concord. It has been presented to John Shaughnessy, State Hazard Mitigation Officer, and Michael Poirier, head of hazard mitigation at NHOEM. It was further referred to Woody Fogg, NHOEM executive head, and Ed Murdough, his deputy. All of them felt that the proposal has great merit, but that no funding was available at NHOEM. It was therefore also presented to Kevin Merli, head of Hazard Mitigation for FEMA's Boston Region (Region I.) The proposal was tried on a pilot basis. Its steps are:

1. A hazard mitigation professional presents SCOPE to each community, city and town in each State, beginning at the State capitol and moving outward in circles.

2. Upon endorsement by the community, city, or town government, a needs assessment is undertaken via a structured questionnaire developed in consultation with various relevant constituencies such as governmental leaders and officials, first responders, emergency management coordinators or directors, and local residents.

3. The results of the structured questionnaires are tabulated into a rough rubric of hazard mitigation needs, in the areas of both natural and societal risks, and then refined via clarification interviews with not only the groups in 2) above, but also new target groups in order to provide an independent system of checks on the work.

4. The second round of results and recommendations from the questionnaires are used as the basis for interviews with all relevant stakeholders, who critique those results.

5. Once a viable set of recommendations emerge from the process, they are prioritized by the responsible governmental officials in each particular venue, and a draft timeline is developed for implementation of the recommendations, the most urgent first.

6. The State emergency management agency, and FEMA, review the recommendations developed in 5) above for consistency with State and Federal hazard mitigation plans.

7. After the completion of the preceding steps, funding possibilities and projections are developed, beginning with the most urgent projects first, and continuing in priority order. Development of the first projects should begin the instant funds are available.

8. At each stage of SCOPE, feedback is presented to the earlier steps and stages, to help ensure that the most current information is being used, and that changes in plans can be made as needed. Those changes are reviewed at local, State, and Federal levels.

SCOPE Proposal revised 2022, All Rights Reserved, Eugene F. Elander

APPENDIX II
ON THE CENTURION PROGRAM:

◆

THE CENTURION PROGRAM:
KEEPING AMERICA SAFE AND SECURE

A Monograph by Eugene F. Elander - Submitted to the U.S Army
War College, 2009

Like liberty, the price of security is eternal vigilance. When it comes to American security, that vital vigilance can be significantly enhanced through implementation of the Centurion Program outlined below. The Centurion Program draws upon sources as diverse as the ancient Roman Republic and Empire, and the modern State of Israel. By going considerably beyond those sources, however, Centurion is innovative and tailored to meet the specific security needs of Twenty-First Century America. The major purposes of Centurion are the enhancement of our ability to cope with the ongoing threats of terrorism against us, along with other societal disasters, and the prevention or mitigation of the results of those threats.

Whatever the failings of the later period of the Roman Empire, its military prowess was legendary for well over a thousand years. The entire known world was conquered by Rome. The Roman forces were organized into units of one hundred troops headed by a Centurion, who supervised smaller sub-units, a system which insured both responsibility and accountability.

The proposed monograph described herein combines the concept of the Centurion with the essential roles today of an effective Home Guard in nations ranging from Israel to China. Several dozen countries today have prominent Home Guards or equivalent reserve forces, and increasingly those forces are used to combat terrorism and other societal threats. America, however, still fails to have that type of Home Guard, a lack which puts us at serious risk. The Centurion Program would remedy that lack, and could be implemented at affordable cost levels. This outline summarizes the full proposal which, if funded, will be presented in a monograph prepared for the U.S. Army War College Strategic Studies Institute.

The essence of the Centurion Program is the recruitment, through a wide variety of measures, of a cadre of one percent of the total United States population, slightly over three million volunteers, to serve as American Centurions. The major goal of these Centurions will be the protection of the American homeland from terrorism, as well as from other societal threats such as mass violence at schools, on public transportation, etc. Not only will this program increase our safety and security significantly, it will also boost our morale by giving so many Americans an opportunity to fight back in a positive manner against terrorism and terror tactics. The feelings of powerlessness in the face of terrorism will be reduced.

That common feeling of helplessness in the wake of the September 11, 2001, attacks damaged our national confidence and will beyond even the direct results of the worst homeland attack in our history. A typical reaction to the present Homeland Security system of color-coded threat levels remains that there is little average Americans can do about such threats. The Centurion Program will provide a meaningful response not only to past terror events, but, even more importantly, a way the public can better cope with likely future terrorism directed against us. The detailed program to be presented in the monograph will cover all aspects of Centurion: funding, structure, recruitment, training, implementation and evaluation.

The genesis for the Centurion concept came from the author's own personal experience as a young boy during World War II. His father, being too old to enlist, served as an Air Raid Warden in Queens, New York, and the author accompanied him on his neighborhood rounds on occasion. Air Raid Wardens ensured that no lights showed to illuminate their neighborhoods, to prevent targeting of bombs from enemy planes based on visual sightings. Participating in air raid prevention meant a great deal to the author. Later, studying Latin and Ancient Rome in High School, the author first began to relate and compare this essential volunteer work during World War II to the Roman Centurions. Now, more than sixty years later, redeveloping the Centurion concept into a volunteer American Home Guard cadre seems reasonable, proper, and vital to our preparedness.

The proposed monograph will specify recruitment methods for Centurion volunteers, various criteria to be applied, training requirements, structure of the volunteer force, chain of command, draft budget, and other considerations. Objections to the concept and its implementation will also be covered. A detailed implementation timeline will be presented, including the steps necessary to make the Centurion Program a reality. Even if the final outcome of Centurion is not in the form proposed in this monograph, some greatly-enhanced Home Guard system is essential to our ability to cope with terrorism and similar threats, now and in the future. Eternal vigilance demands Centurion.

APPENDIX III
– First Op-Ed on Russian Invasion of Ukraine
(written and submitted worldwide immediately after it began)

◆

<u>DECLARE RUSSIAN LEADER VLADIMIR PUTIN A WAR CRIMINAL NOW!</u> Op-Ed by Dr. Eugene F. Elander, USA/Sweden

Now that Russian Leader Vladimir Putin has carried out his threat of attacking the independent sovereign nation of Ukraine, as one more step in Putin's atrocious plan to restore former Soviet Union territorial goals – while grossly weakening not only Western Europe and NATO, but all democracies, everywhere – the time has come to formally declare Vladimir Putin an international war criminal, subject to prosecution by all jurisdictions, including proper courts in The Hague. Putin will thus join the ranks of despicable disgraced despots such as Ugandan dictator Idi Amin and Serbian atrocity-perpetrator Slobodan Milosevic. This horrific invasion cannot be tolerated!

This author's preference would have been for emergency admission of Ukraine as a provisional NATO (North Atlantic Treaty Organization) member as soon as Putin's deranged threats began, but no such consideration has occurred. Meanwhile, as the United Nations and all responsible world leaders condemn this tragic Russian invasion, only one public figure seems to endorse it: the twice-impeached former U.S. President Donald J. Trump, who now boasts of his friendship with and support for Putin and such dictators as North Korean leader Kim Jong Un. Shame!

We must understand what is at stake here: it is not just the fate of Ukraine, an independent nation; rather, it is the fate of democracy itself and of the entire post-WWII world order! There is little to be gained by re-hashing how the present crisis might well have been prevented, such as by taking far stronger sanctions against Russia's Putin with his 2014 theft of Ukraine's Crimean Peninsula, supposedly on behalf of its Russian-speaking residents. Undoubtedly, the fact that Putin got away with that gross violation of an independent nation's territorial integrity encouraged him to go very much further; it is highly likely that Putin's present goals go far beyond Ukraine, and that he is attempting to re-build the territory of the former Soviet Union.

Declaring Vladimir Putin to be an international war criminal furthers not only the twin causes of justice and democracy; equally important is the strategic role of such a declaration in repudiating not only Putin's atrocious misbehavior by invading Ukraine, but also by undercutting his further ambitions of re-creating the much-enlarged territory of the former Soviet Union. *What next: will Poland or Lithuania, or even our family homes on Gotland, Sweden, be attacked by Putin?*

This atrocious theft of independent territory should have been stopped with Crimea in 2014; <u>it must be stopped, now and forever. International war criminal Vladimir Putin must be brought to justice, now and forever; that will be the strongest sanction of all!</u> *If Western Democracies do not hang together for Ukraine now, we will all surely hang separately later.*

APPENDIX IV
– Further Op-Ed On Invasion of Ukraine
(written and submitted after first 100 days of Russia's War)

TURNING THE TIDE OF TERROR IN UKRAINE!
URGENT OP-ED by Dr. Eugene F. Elander, Visby, Gotland, Sweden
June 4, 2022

Now that more than three months have passed since Russian President Vladimir Putin's misbegotten horrid invasion of the neighboring nation of Ukraine, the entire civilized world is left to wonder why no effective preventive action has been taken. Such international bodies such as the United Nations, the International Courts, and mutual defense groups such as NATO, appear powerless to halt total destruction of the independent sovereign nation of Ukraine, thus sending a horrid signal to other expansive powers that literal murder and mayhem will unfortunately be tolerated.

This tragic lack of effective preventive action regarding Ukraine stems from the tragic mis-definition of the destruction of Ukraine as being an act of war, when it is clearly international terrorism! Valid wars have some goal beyond the horrid destruction of a sovereign nation; wars often even have some pretense of being honorable; wars have some rules and limits as to tactics, weapons, treatment of non-combatants, and humanitarian relief. The Ukraine invasion meets none of these standards; it is rather a set of wrongful and illegal acts taken by a deranged leader who enthusiastically violates a host of international laws and protections. Yet our authorized international bodies are ineffective at stopping these grave acts.

The civilized world needs to properly define Vladimir Putin's invasion of Ukraine as just what it is: **international terrorism,** rather than war – thus calling for action which will effectively halt that invasion at once by removing or blocking its sole source: Vladimir Putin himself. The invasion of Ukraine is not being conducted by Putin as president of Russia – it is rather being conducted by a prime terrorist who happens, in this instance, to also head a nation. The Russian nation and people are not the source of the atrocities in Ukraine: intentional destruction of so many cities, intentional killings of so many civilians, including men, women, and children; the intentional acts of mass murder, looting, maiming, raping, and abusing innocents. These and other atrocities are not acts of war; they are clearly Putin terror tactics.

AUTHOR BIOGRAPHY:
Eugene F. Elander

5350 Hermitage Avenue, Valley Village CA 91607
678-599-0240 elandersbe@gmail.com

◆

Eugene F. Elander

Dr. Eugene Elander won the Young Poets Award at 16 from the Dayton, Ohio Poets Guild for his poem *The Vision*. He was chosen Poet Laureate of Pownal, Vermont, for his poem *Pownal People*, and was a leading contender for the post of Poet Laureate of Rochester, New Hampshire. His three new verses titled *America the Beautiful: September 11, 2001*, memorializing the terrorist tragedy, have been widely acclaimed and were read into the Congressional Record by then Connecticut U.S. Senator, Chris Dodd.

Dr. Elander has authored four volumes of poetry: *The Right Click, The World Click, Journeyings*, and *Philosophy over Fika* (two of which were co-authored with his wife Birgit), as well as two published novels: *The Goat of God*, and *Turning the Tides*. His self-help book titled *Empowerment: Taking Charge of your Life* was completed and published via Amazon KDP (Kindle Direct Publishing). In Summer, 2018, Dr. Elander finished *My Many Miracles: A Spiritual Journey*, published by Lang Book Publishing and available also through Amazon.com and other sources. His most recent book, *Animal Tales: Confessions of a*

Humane Investigator/ACO, the true story of his years handling cases of animal abuse, neglect, and cruelty, was published by Humanities Academic Publishers of California in 2023. His auto-biography, ***Never Give In, Never Give Up: a Memoir of Hope,*** is awaiting publication in 2023.

Several other books by Dr. Elander are underway, including a public version of his doctoral thesis on ***Cooperatism***, a new economic system he designed which includes all stakeholders (workers, consumers, and the public as well as stockholders) in crucial decision-making by firms. Dr. Elander is an original member of the Stonepile Writers group in North Georgia, affiliated with the University of North Georgia, which has anthologized a number of his poems; and a former member of the Poetry Society of New Hampshire. He is an Op-Ed contributor to various progressive causes, news media & websites and a freelance columnist who published an award-winning newspaper for ten years in New London, CT. He is president of Elander Press, which edits works and advises aspiring authors; and of economic consulting firm Elander Enterprises,

Professionally, Dr. Elander is an economist and college lecturer; and has served as an agency executive director, emergency management consultant, investigator; and former animal control officer, deputy code enforcement and health officer for Town of Farmington, New Hampshire. He continues to teach and tutor on-line writing, economics and business, and research courses.

He and wife Birgit divide their time between Southern California and her homeland, Gotland, Sweden. They have also traveled extensively throughout North America and Europe, and have children and grandchildren in Connecticut, Georgia, Minneapolis, Los Angeles, and Gotland.

www.ingramcontent.com/pod-product-compliance
Lightning Source LLC
LaVergne TN
LVHW051232080426
835513LV00016B/1546